WRITING
TO BE
UNDERSTOOD

What Works and Why

Cuesta Park Consulting

WRITING TO BE UNDERSTOOD:
What Works and Why

Copyright © 2018 Anne Janzer

Cuesta Park Consulting

Cuesta Park Consulting
Mountain View, California

Printed in the United States of America

Hardcover ISBN: 978-0-9996248-1-4
Paperback ISBN: 978-0-9996248-2-1

CONTENTS

INTRODUCTION

Can you name your favorite nonfiction books—the ones that explain complicated topics or shift your perspective while holding your interest?

If you're always prowling the nonfiction lists for undiscovered gems or leafing through magazines for fresh and fascinating topics, then you know the joy of reading a book, blog post, or article, and gaining new insights about the world. Sometimes you encounter answers to niggling questions you didn't realize you had.

You also know the disappointment of diving into an article or book with high hopes, only to get lost, confused, or bored partway through, putting it aside with resignation and the thought that life is too short.

What's going on here? Why are certain writers so effective at connecting with us and explaining complicated and unfamiliar topics, while others leave us cold?

Clearly, individual tastes come into play. Your list of favorite authors, journalists, and explainers won't match mine. Skim the Amazon reviews of any best seller and you'll find that *no* author resonates with every reader.

Yet some writers delight a broad audience, even when covering fields like finance, astrophysics, cognitive science, or medicine. They are masters at explaining complicated topics to non-expert readers. We cherish those writers who guide us through the unknown; they become friends and teachers we return to for insight.

What makes their writing different? Why does it connect with us? And how can we, as writers, try to be more like them?

What Works

Determining what "works" in writing is a highly subjective exercise. To paraphrase the famous saying about pornography, I can't define effective writing, but I know it when I read it.

In doing the research for this book, I started by surveying the writers *I* find particularly engaging and successful. A few are specialists in their fields who succeed at writing accessible books for a general audience; others are journalists or nonfiction authors who specialize in explaining complexity for the rest of us. Were these writers simply born with exceptional written communication skills? Probably not.

What if we could join their ranks, or at least get closer to their results?

I dissected these authors' writing strategies to tease out what they did. To offset my own biases, I interviewed many nonfiction lovers about their strategies and favorite writers. Despite the diversity of styles and subject matters represented, the same methods and techniques appeared repeatedly: stories, explanatory analogies, skillful use of details, figurative language, repetition, and more.

Could it be that simple? To use a term from the technology industry, could we reverse-engineer effective nonfiction writing?

I don't think it's quite that easy.

It's Not About the Words

A piece of writing succeeds or fails not on the page but in a reader's head. To increase the impact of your nonfiction writing, focus beyond the words and topic, on the minds of the readers.

If you have spent years agonizing over word choices and polishing prose, this advice may trigger an uncomfortable shift in perspective. It's humbling or distressing to think that those words you have slaved over may have slid right past glazed-over eyes. Your success depends on other people's comprehension.

To visualize this concept, imagine a Venn diagram for your writing topic, with two overlapping circles. One circle contains the ideas or topics you want to communicate, and the other contains those topics that your readers are interested in right now, at this moment.

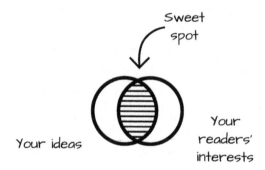

The circles overlap in your content *sweet spot*. This is the logical starting point for your writing.

If the intersection is large and *everyone* wants to read about your topic, you are either exceptionally lucky or deluded:

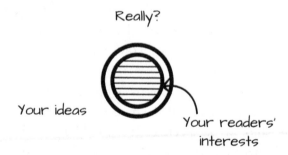

If you don't see any overlap, try a different approach. Think deeply about the readers' situations and their needs, adjust your target audience, or switch topics.

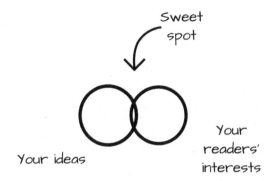

If, as is often the case, the intersection of your enthu-siasm and the readers' interests is a narrow sliver, don't worry. *Skillful writers expand the sweet spot as they write.* They do this by understanding what's going on in the readers' heads.

Why Good Writing Works

When assessing *why* a piece of nonfiction makes an impact, we should start with what happens during reading. I don't pretend to have all the answers, but I sure have a lot of questions. For example:

- Why does an apt metaphor help you understand or remember a topic?
- Why do you space out when reading about ab-stract concepts, and how can writers alleviate that mental fatigue?
- Why do you unthinkingly push back against or re-ject certain ideas, and how can writers get around that resistance?

This book grew from my attempts to answer these questions. I've explored cognitive science topics and posed questions to experts in fields such as psychology, comedy, journalism, and logical reasoning, who have generously shared their advice and perspectives in these pages. I've looked at the works of successful nonfiction authors, and tried a lot of the advice in my own writing.

In the chapters that follow, we'll explore the challenges and techniques of nonfiction writing, particularly when writing to explain. We'll examine what's happening with the reader, theorize about why specific writing techniques work, and delve into ways that you can implement these methods in your own work.

Who Should Read This Book

Because my success as a writer depends on *you*, the reader, let's start with a few basic assumptions. Specifically, I'm assuming that you're either a nonfiction writer seeking to explain things or someone who loves reading this kind of work. Either way, you're curious about what makes the best writers so effective.

If you struggle to get the attention of readers or are writing for an audience other than your peers, this book will help. If you make your living as a writer translating between specialists and general audiences, you will discover the theory behind common writing techniques so that you can use them more effectively.

At its core, this book serves nonfiction writers who seek to explain complicated topics outside of the comfort and familiarity of a particular industry or academic discipline. It is dedicated to those who work in the messy trenches of the real world, where people skim an article on a mobile phone while riding the subway, or pick up a book in a few spare minutes of the day.

When you're writing for a general audience, you have no built-in control over the reader. Academics can *assign* reading to students and test their comprehension of it. When you are writing for the world at large, readers may spend only a few seconds to decide whether to pick up (or click through to) your writing, and a few moments more to determine if it's worth their scarce attention.

Your words are all you have; learn how to use them to their greatest effect.

For writers, you're an ideal audience for this book if:

- You know your stuff. Your topics may be complicated and knotty, but you know them well.

- You can write. We won't talk about grammar or sentence structure here, although you will find a discussion of tone and style in Part Three. SCOTT ADAMS POST/CHAPTER

- You care about connecting with readers and sharing your knowledge or your message. Instead of sounding smart or demonstrating your expertise, you desire to be understood by others.

The tools and methods in this book can help you make your writing more effective, reaching more people or connecting more deeply. In short, you can learn to emulate the nonfiction authors you most admire.

How to Use This Book

Every writer can learn and hone the skills of compelling communication. By focusing on your audience's needs and applying the practices of effective writing, you can transform your own style and approach.

Considering that the topic is writing, you may be surprised by the amount of cognitive science in this book. That's because the end goal is being *understood*, and understanding is a cognitive function.

Part One begins with strategies and methods for understanding the audience needs and context. Because the chapters in Part One create the foundation for the subsequent sections, I'd suggest that you at least skim this section and the context for your writing.

The chapters in Part Two discuss writing tactics and the challenges of explaining abstract topics. We'll examine techniques for writing about abstractions, the power of analogy and storytelling to communicate complex interactions, and the use of repetition to reinforce understanding.

You also have to hold the reader's attention. Masterful communicators make esoteric subjects interesting for the rest of us. The chapters in Part Three include advice for enlivening your writing through imagery, tone and style, humility, and humor.

Each chapter covers both the why and how of the various writing methods. Big, juicy topics like humor and storytelling deserve deeper study than I can provide. The discussions here are meant to inspire you to experiment with these techniques and to lower the barriers to getting started. Even a dash of humor or a snippet of story can help readers absorb your message.

Humor
storytelling

Simply reading this book won't make you a better writer. If only it were that easy! By exploring and practicing the methods in this book, you can expand your skill set and develop a writing style that reaches more people.

Why It Matters

Many brilliant people struggle to communicate outside of their core audiences. We see evidence of this problem on a daily basis. Climate scientists run into barriers of beliefs when explaining events in their fields. Technologists describe the next disruption without sensing discomfort or confusion in their readers. Policymakers frame discussions in terms that don't make sense to the average voter or that obscure the human impact of critical decisions.

As the world grows ever more complex, we need people who write and speak across industry and genre boundaries, who incite our curiosity and show us the truths we should see. We need people who communicate across chasms in beliefs and understanding, healing the divisiveness that characterizes current public debate.

Journalists once filled this role for the average reader, yet they are under pressure from changing business models. We cannot rely on journalism alone, nor can we reserve important messages and ideas for the shrinking population of readers with the time or focus to do deep, scholarly reading.

We need more effective communicators—starting with you.

PART ONE

UNDERSTANDING
YOUR READERS

1

WHO ARE YOUR READERS?

How choosing a narrow audience can broaden your reach
Why finding points of connection makes readers more receptive
How to choose a specific audience

Although language is still pretty recent in an evolutionary context, it has been with humans for millennia, shaping our brains and behaviors. As individuals, most of us have been learning from and sharing with other people our entire lives. Each of us carries within us enormous amounts of working knowledge about how to communicate.

Think about it for a moment. You automatically adopt different explanatory styles based on the person you are addressing. If a three-year-old asks you how your phone works, you'll give a different answer than you would to an adult colleague. Faced with someone returning to civilization after two decades in the wilderness, you'd come up with a different approach altogether. You automatically make decisions and shift your explanations based on what you know about the other person, as well as real-time feedback such as questions or confused expressions.

Yet when we write, those absent readers become less real to us, and we lose the benefit of a lifetime of acquired skills. We become entranced with our own words or caught up in our subject and write for ourselves or for some faceless, anonymous "general public." Everybody suffers when this happens.

To improve your nonfiction writing, first bring the reader back into the equation. When you picture a real person, you can activate that almost-instinctive knowledge you've acquired about communicating.

The Unknown Reader

While it may feel like a one-way street, writing does not fulfill its purpose until someone reads and understands the words.

Remember the Venn diagram in the introduction: what *you* want to write, and what *the reader* needs to see?

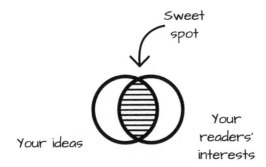

To find the area of overlap, you must understand the reader's needs and context. For many writers, this is the most pressing and difficult problem to solve.

So, who's *your* reader?

If you've honed your writing skills in an academic context, this question may be easy to answer. Whether writing papers for classes or peer-reviewed journal articles, you have a fairly accurate sense of the audience, including their background knowledge and why they're reading your work. The same holds true when you write for people in your industry; you understand their roles and needs.

This background knowledge is missing when you address a general, unknown audience. The potential world of readers is as broad and wide as the ocean. Authors who are expert in their fields can fall prey to one of two conflicting temptations in this situation:

- They stick to writing for readers they know, such as colleagues or people like them. Academic researchers who present dense, scholarly works to a general audience limit the potential scope and impact of their efforts.

- Conversely, they may attempt to write for everyone, assuming that the reader brings nothing to the conversation. This approach often results in a generic, dull description that interests no one.

No matter how compelling you find your topic, you won't reach everyone—that's a given. The more specific you are in visualizing the target reader, the more effectively you can write. Put aside your fascination with the subject and pick a target audience.

Pick an Audience, Any Audience

Thinking of a specific person activates your built-in communication skills, using your life-long training in human interaction to make decisions about the writing. Knowing your reader influences the words you choose, the sentences you craft, and even the approach you use to present your ideas.

Many writers make the common mistake of being too vague when picturing a reader. When it comes to identifying a target audience: *everyone* is *no one.*

You may worry about excluding other people if you write specifically for one individual. Relax—that doesn't necessarily happen. A well-defined audience simplifies decisions about explanations and word choice. Your style may become more distinctive, in a way that attracts people beyond the target reader.

Andy Weir wrote *The Martian* for science fiction readers who want their stories firmly grounded in scientific fact, and perhaps rocket scientists who enjoy science fiction. I belong to neither audience, yet I enjoyed the book. Weir was so successful at pleasing his target audience that they shared it widely and enthusiastically. Because Weir didn't try to cater to *everyone*, he wrote something that delighted his core audience. Eventually, his work traveled far beyond that sphere.

It may be counterintuitive, but if you want to reach a larger audience, consider concentrating more closely on a specific segment of it. To broaden your impact, tighten your focus on the reader.

Once you've chosen a target reader or two, make a list of the identities, beliefs, or experiences you may have in common. Particularly when you're trying to reach people outside your field, or readers with different beliefs, these connection points offer clues as to how to proceed to earn and sustain the readers' attention.

Forging a Shared Identity with the Reader

In the Prologue of her memoir, *Lab Girl*, Hope Jahren starts by asking you (the reader) to look out the window and contemplate a leaf on a tree. After discussing possible factors to explore (its shape, color, veins, and more), she prompts you to pose a specific question about your leaf. Then she makes a surprising assertion.[1]

> Guess what? You are now a scientist. People will tell you that you have to know math to be a scientist, or physics, or chemistry... What comes first is a question, and you're already there.

Because you asked a question, you are a scientist and one of her colleagues—and therefore have stake in her story.

We get so caught up in our subjects, we often forget about the readers. When writing about sensitive or challenging subjects, the readers may be the most important part of the story. People who feel they share something in common with you are more likely to be open to your ideas.

In 2016, a team of researchers led by the Harvard School of Education surveyed ninth-grade teachers and students in a large, suburban high school in the U.S. More than 300 students and 25 teachers answered a series of questions as part of a psychological study disguised as a "getting to know you" exercise. After receiving the questionnaires, the researchers gave students and teachers alike feedback (manipulated, of course) about their shared characteristics and preferences. Some were told they aligned on three key points, others on five.

The researchers checked back five weeks later, asking students and teachers alike about their experiences so far. Those teachers and students who were told they shared five points of connection reported better relationships, while students earned higher grades.[2]

Human beings come with built-in us/them filtering. Family members are our closest groups, followed by community members, work colleagues, citizens of cities or states, and so on. We also sort and categorize people by behavior and appearance: those who look like us, dress like us, behave like us, root for the same sports teams, worship in the same way, etc.

When we first meet someone, we instinctively look for ways that we are the same or different. We're not aware of many of these us/them filters. Deep in our primitive minds, we are trying to determine if the person poses a threat.

Despite our strong need to form groups, people also shift identities and switch between roles quickly: parent, child, sibling, work colleague, singer in the choir, member of the neighborhood, etc.

Our social identities are fluid.

When reading fiction or nonfiction, we virtually inhabit different groups, perspectives, and identities. So, take your readers' roles and identity into consideration when writing.

For complicated or global topics, you may choose to reframe the reader's sense of belonging from a smaller group to a broader one. The famous Blue Marble photo of the Earth from the Apollo 17 space flight altered our perspectives. Rather than being members of neighborhoods, cities, and nations, we saw at a glance the larger group made up of the inhabitants of this globe. For a moment, at least, viewers experienced a shared global identity.

Even as you define a target audience and understand their differences, remember the roles and identities you share. That perspective will be invaluable if you want to forge a stronger connection with the absent reader.

Methods for Writers:
Identifying Your Audience

Spend some time thinking about your ideal audience, the people you most want to address with your writing. To help you narrow in on reader profiles, borrow a practice from marketing.

Identify ideal readers

In the technology industry, where I spent my career, businesses create *buyer personas*, or detailed profiles of buyers and decision-makers. Personas begin with job titles and add general demographic and psychographic information, such as attitudes and aspirations, to create a fictional character who represents a segment of buyers. Armed with this insight, marketers generate content to meet the needs of specific groups of prospects and customers.

Persona development forces marketers to contemplate customer needs and context rather than the thing they are selling. Writers can benefit from doing something similar.

Choose a few "ideal readers" for your work. Come up with specific examples of individuals you would like to reach. Aiming for a market segment isn't enough. We don't write for data or segments—we write for *people*. Picturing an individual (whether fictional or real) connects with your innate social instincts, guiding decisions about what to include, what style to adopt, and which stories might resonate.

If you're not sure of your ideal audience, start by selecting people based on their backgrounds and motivation for reading. For example, you might start with:

- People who read the *New York Times* and are interested in housing policy
- Educated baby boomers seeking to understand the recent advances in medicine that are relevant to their lives

Then find real or fictional characters that fit in those categories. When you can envision a specific individual, you can start to call on cognitive empathy—the subject of the next chapter.

Look for shared experiences and identities

Michelle Tillis Lederman, author of *The 11 Laws of Likability*, coaches corporate executives and nonprofit leaders to connect with others through shared experiences: "Realizing we share a connection with someone else puts us at ease." According to Lederman, "When we find one place of agreement, it's easier to get to the next place of agreement. For example, we might present a universally acceptable objective, such as ridding the world of cancer, while acknowledging controversy over the mechanisms that we to reach that objective. Even if we're not on the same page about *how*, we agree on *why*."

Three rules to remember

These are my three essential rules for choosing your ideal reading audience:

1. Your audience is never "everyone." Writing for everyone pleases no one.

2. Having a specific audience makes your writing better.

3. Personas, demographic classifications, and customer segments aren't people. Write for people.

Writing Advice
from a Best-Selling Nonfiction Author

Name: Daniel Pink

Experience: Author of six bestselling nonfiction books

Specific Skill Set: Writing effectively about complicated topics for a wide audience

---

Daniel Pink writes about topics ranging from neuroscience to human motivation to chronobiology, explaining these subjects for the general reading public. His books rise quickly to the top of nonfiction best seller lists and stay there for months. Plus, they are always a pleasure to read.

How does he cover these geeky topics while making them appealing to a broad audience? I asked him. It turns out that he applies many of the writing practices described in this book, while focusing relentlessly on the needs of his audience.

Identifying his ideal audience

Says Pink, "I write for readers who want to understand big ideas and findings but who aren't experts. I do the time-consuming work of figuring stuff out so they don't have to. What's more, one of my own tests of whether I understand a concept is whether I can explain it quickly and clearly to someone who knows little about the subject."

Getting outside opinions

To write for others effectively, we have to get outside our own heads. Pink does this extensively during the idea-generation phase. "When it comes to generating and testing ideas, I like to talk to people—to bounce notions off of them, get their reactions, have them find weak spots."

How about during the writing process? "In the writing itself, my circle is quite small. The most important reader is my wife, who is also my business partner. She reads every word I write—often multiple times. She is an extremely sharp-minded and astute reader who—and this is important—doesn't shy away from telling me I'm not making sense. My book editor, too, plays an enormous role in both talking through ideas and reading and editing pages."

Balancing story and data

In each of his books, Pink draws readers in with stories and anecdotes told well. *When* begins with the launch of the *Lusitania*. *Drive* begins with monkeys unexpectedly solving puzzles. I asked him how he found the balance of story, data, and exposition. His response: "I don't aim for specific ratios. But I think hard about what combination is the best way to get across an idea. Sometimes doing that requires leaning more heavily on one particular element. Also, the balance is sometimes dictated by the quality of the material. If I've got a great story, I'll use that and supplement with research. If I've got a mind-boggling study, I might rely less heavily on the story and let the findings speak for themselves."

Other important writing advice

What other advice does he offer to nonfiction writers?

"Three things. Rewrite. Rewrite. Rewrite."

2

THE ABSENT READER

Why writers need cognitive empathy
Your reader isn't entirely rational—and neither are you
How improv develops empathy for the reader

When we converse with another person, we receive real-time feedback into whether or not that person understands us (if we bother to pay attention.)

In a face-to-face conversation, we can detect when the listener's interest flags. We see them reaching surreptitiously for their phones or their eyes glazing over. Perhaps a puzzled expression makes us pause, giving the listener a chance to ask a question. When writing, however, we lack those cues, so we have to understand and empathize with someone who is not actually in front of us.

How can we train ourselves to think about that absent reader and their needs? We need to develop empathy for people who are not present.

Empathy for the Reader

People throw around the word *empathy* loosely, so let's distinguish between a couple of variations on the term.

Cognitive empathy refers to the ability to take another person's perspective. When someone says, "I see where you are coming from," they are claiming cognitive empathy.

Affective empathy is the ability to summon the appropriate emotional response for another person's emotional state. The common refrain for affective empathy is "I feel your pain."

Writers don't have to feel or directly respond to readers' emotions, but they should at least have a sense of the readers' feelings. As an obvious example, if you're writing about end-of-life care, you're aware that readers inhabit highly emotional environments. But if you're writing about technology advances, you would want to know if the audience approaches technological or behavior change fearfully. That insight would change the way you write.

As a writer, cognitive empathy helps you understand readers' perspectives: what they already know and need to know, what they are doing when they encounter this information. And while you do not need to feel their pains, you should consider the emotional context.

What's Going On in the Reader's Brain

Most nonfiction writers operate in the realm of the rational, analytical thought. The reasoning mind is a wonderful thing. All around us, we see evidence of the miraculous results of human reasoning and problem solving: airplanes that appear to defy gravity, medicines that cure unseen illnesses, or manipulation of matter at the atomic level.

Yet, always remember that human thought is a complex combination of abstract thought, linear thinking, associative processes, emotions, sensory perceptions, mental shortcuts, and ephemeral memories. You are not an entirely rational being. Nor is your reader. By planting yourself firmly in the field of rationality and ignoring emotion, you reduce the effectiveness of your writing.

Numerous psychological studies have proven the link between emotion, learning, and memory.[3] Ignore emotion at your own peril. Even as you attempt to engage the analytical part of your reader's brain, you won't go far without bringing the rest of those mental processes along with you.

If you want to change someone's opinion or influence their behavior, then it's even *more* critical that you understand what's going on beyond the analytical mind.

At the risk of vastly oversimplifying a complex field, let's create a working model of the reader's brain, labeling a few cognitive functions for later reference. This isn't a neurobiology textbook, so I'll refrain from too much anatomical mapping.

Sensory systems interpret the sight, sound, touch, and other senses. These systems activate even when we *think* about seeing, touching, moving, or hearing things.

Reasoning systems include the prefrontal cortex and other regions of the brain that manage language, symbols, and abstractions. We identify with our reasoning systems, believing (usually in error) that they control our decisions and behavior. But the reasoning mind isn't always rational. Behavioral economists demonstrate that when we make decisions, we frequently rely on unreliable shortcuts and then rationalize our choices after the fact. So, we are less rational and analytical than we may believe. If you're familiar with Daniel Kahneman's *Thinking Fast and Slow*, I'm including both his System 1 (fast and intuitive) and System 2 (slow and analytical) in the description of the reasoning systems.

Emotional systems use evolutionarily older parts of the brain, including the limbic systems. Some emotions run pretty deep. As writers, we should understand that our words and images prompt emotional reactions that may affect the reader's receptivity to a particular topic.

Further back in time and lower in the brain you'll find the *amygdala*, an ancient structure that manages the quick responses that keep us alive in times of threat. It's home to the "fight or flight" instinct. Emotions related to the amygdala (fear, disgust, etc.) kick in quickly, before rational thought has a chance to work.

The act of reading may operate on many levels in the reader's mind: visual and language processing systems parse the words, visual or sensory systems again imagine what the person is reading, reasoning systems assess the content. The limbic (emotional) systems may respond to the ideas *or* to the writer personally. A reader who feels threatened might have an active amygdala response as well.

You are writing for the reader's entire mind, not just the rational parts. I'm not saying that you should overtly *manipulate* people, but if you want to be effective in reaching your audience, understand how and why readers react to your writing. You can explain things to the rational reader, but to make an impact, appeal to other layers of the reader's mind.

Connecting on Multiple Levels

The most effective writers don't simply explain things— they make their ideas memorable. They leverage innate communication skills to connect with other people.

Having a clear understanding of your audience makes you a more effective writer. To use the writing methods and techniques described in Parts Two and Three, start with an understanding of the reader. Take the reader's perspective.

Writers apply different techniques and strategies for reminding themselves about the reader, so as to activate cognitive empathy.

- Many people visualize their ideal readers when drafting.
- A few paste pictures of target audience members on their walls.
- Others try out topics or ideas on existing groups of colleagues, students, family members, or strangers at parties. (I've done that last one.)

If you struggle with perspective taking, consider signing up for an improvisational comedy class. Surprisingly, doing collaborative, improvised skits with others can make you a better writer.

Although he is best known for his acting skills, Alan Alda has dedicated years to the cause of improving scientific communication. This mission started with a gig he had hosting the PBS television series *Scientific American Frontiers* for eleven years. Doing this, he confronted the challenges of communicating effectively about scientific topics to a general television-viewing audience.

In his book *If I Understood You, Would I Have This Look on My Face?*, Alda describes how he realized that improvisational acting techniques could help scientists communicate more effectively. (In addition to being a talented actor, Alda is also an engaging writer. It doesn't seem entirely fair, does it?)

It makes sense. Improvisation requires that actors focus intently on their scene partners to follow what's happening. The two cardinal rules of improv are saying *yes, and…* to any situation offered you, and always making your partner look good. These are worthwhile skills. Writes Alda, "Developing empathy and learning to recognize what the other person is thinking are both essential to good communication."

Alda didn't stop at applying this insight to his own television work. He joined up with Stony Brook University in New York and lent his name to the Alan Alda Center for Communicating Science, where training and research continues in this intersection of empathy and scientific or medical communication. He and the team at the Alda Center devised the Alda Method™ for Science Communication.

In addition to conducting research into scientific communication, the Center holds workshops and training for professionals in science, technology, and medical fields. Says Laura Lindenfeld, director of the Alda Center, "Our mission is to train scientists and medical professionals to communicate with empathy, warmth, and clarity." The Center takes its workshops on the road, around the country and around the globe.

In workshops featuring the Alda Method, participants learn the basics of improvisation and practice exercises that help them relate to their scene partners. They might toss imaginary balls of varying weights to other participants, or do a mirroring exercise to come up with the same words at the same time as their partners. While those activities have little to do with science or medicine, they have *everything* to do with thinking deeply about your partner in a dialogue or conversation.

Says Lindenfeld, "The beauty of improv is that it helps you to understand something about the person communicating with you, and forces you to listen and consider their questions. Improv also has a rule about making your partner look good, which is a valuable attitude to bring to any interaction that includes potential disagreement."

The Alda Center curriculum first develops face-to-face communication and speaking skills. It then builds on this interpersonal training to enhance written communications, such as blogging, grant proposals, and opinion pieces.

I had to ask Lindenfeld: How do improv classes apply to writing skills? She answered: "Principally, the same things that make you a good speaker make you a good writer. It has to do with your relationship with the audience. Communication is about being present with your audience—whether it's a real one standing before you or a virtual audience that you imagine. The initial, face-to-face form of training helps people establish a strong sense that they are communicating *with* someone rather than *at* them. It is through this process that the training translates so well to writing. We ask our students to imagine their audience, what's at stake for them, and why they would care."

Improvisational exercises develop cognitive empathy, which fuels better communication with your reader. But they're not the only way to build up your interpersonal skills. Simply conversing with others can improve your overall empathy. Sherry Turkle, professor of Social Studies of Science and Technology at the Massachusetts Institute of Technology (MIT), suggests that while our technological devices may be eroding empathy, human conversation can reverse this trend. "To the disconnections of our over-connected world, I argue that conversation is the talking cure."[4]

Cognitive empathy is a natural response to another person's perspective. Visualizing readers, talking to people, and taking improv classes are all ways to develop and refine this aptitude.

Methods for Writers:
Getting to Know Your Readers

To develop cognitive empathy for your reader, use a two-pronged approach: get in front of real people, and then ponder their needs when they are absent. Here are a few strategies.

Engage in a conversation about your topic

Hold a workshop, and talk with people directly. If you're a teacher, give a lecture and welcome questions. Corner someone at a neighborhood gathering.

Or, find a friend or colleague who can serve as a proxy or stand-in for your ideal reader. This might be someone in the same role or with a similar personality type who understands the target audience well.

Do whatever it takes to test your message with other people and see how people respond. Do their eyes light up? Are they confused? What specific words do they use when asking questions? What resonates with them?

This tactic only works if you pay attention to the other person. Make yourself pause during your delivery. Take a breath, slow down and watch the other person.

If your listener finds an excuse to slip away when you stop talking—well, they've just provided valuable input, even if it's painful. If that person belongs to your core audience, you may need to tailor your message.

Ask questions about the reader's context

When other people aren't present, imagine their needs, feelings, and context. Try answering a few questions about a typical reader you'd like to reach.

- How will they feel about the topic? Answering this question requires that you inhabit, for a moment, your reader's perspective. It's an exercise in cognitive empathy or perspective taking, and can yield invaluable clues that will help you write more effectively.

- How much will they trust you as a source? Will they find this information as the result of an Internet search, or will a trusted colleague, physician, or friend give it to them? If they might approach your words with a sense of skepticism or caution, you'll need to establish your credibility without sounding self-important.

- Will your writing appear within the context of a class? If so, most readers will bring a certain openness of mind and willingness to give your words a chance. You can lead with a story, and have faith they won't bail out immediately.

- Will they encounter this piece of writing as one more thing to do in a busy day? If so, you'll have to earn their attention—inspire them to find something useful and bookmark it for further reading.

- What's their motivation for reading? Do they hope to confirm their own opinions? Satisfy curiosity? Advance their careers? Are they suffering from a disease or facing a difficult dilemma, and searching for solutions?

- Do they need a quick answer? If so, what are their questions? Anticipate and answer their questions up front, then go into the "how and why" of your answers.

Your answers to these questions will guide decisions about what information to include and how to present it. If you're not sure of the answers, make a guess and move forward.

Simply thinking about the reader in depth has already enhanced your cognitive empathy. If you plan to continue writing on the topic, make a point of interacting with readers after you have published. Read the reviews and talk to people about the ideas in the text. The insight you gain can help you be more effective with your *next* work.

Write yourself a letter

Write a letter to yourself from your ideal reader, with all the questions you think they might ask. This forces you to take the other person's perspective.

Rules to remember

- Your success depends on the reader, so understand their needs.
- If possible, talk to people who resemble your ideal readers.
- If your readers aren't available, do the next best thing and imagine their needs and situations.

3

HOW MUCH DO THEY NEED TO KNOW?

The curse of knowledge
Balancing width and breadth
The perils of oversimplification

Few of your readers care about what you know, no matter how many years you have spent accumulating that wisdom. They care about what *they* need or want to understand.

You share much in common with your readers: you both live a world with numerous, competing demands on your attention, limited time for "deep reading," and perhaps a longing for simplicity and clarity.

How do you provide the right amount of information without either oversimplifying the subject or overloading the reader? You'll have to decide what to include and what to leave out. The more you love your subject, the harder this decision can be.

Beware the Curse of Knowledge

Think of a well-known, familiar song, like "Happy Birthday" or "Jingle Bells." Sing it to yourself in your head. Then, find a friend and ask them to guess the song as you tap out its rhythm.

You won't expect them to get it right away, but you might be surprised and frustrated by how long it takes them to correctly guess the tune rattling around in your head. At least, that's what psychologist Elizabeth Newton found when she tested this very thing.

In 1990, Newton was a graduate student in psychology at Stanford University. She conducted an experiment in which half of the participants (the tappers) were asked to tap out the rhythms of common songs, while the other half (the listeners) guessed the songs. The tappers estimated how long it would take the listeners to name the right tune.[5]

The people tapping were inevitably surprised by the listeners' inability to hear the tune that matched the rhythm. It seemed obvious to the tappers. This study illustrates a phenomenon known as the *curse of knowledge*, or the challenge of getting out of our own heads.

Once we know something, it's difficult to remember *not* knowing it. We take our knowledge for granted.

We can spot *other* people suffering from the curse of knowledge pretty easily. We've all seen it:

- The physician who speaks in medical terms you don't know
- The academic author who writes a paper, intended for a general audience, filled with terms that only a graduate student would understand

These people aren't trying to hoodwink or confuse you. They simply forget that you don't know what they know.

It's much harder to detect symptoms of this tendency in our *own* behavior. When smart, caring people write incomprehensible stuff, the curse of knowledge is usually to blame. It plagues experts who write for the layperson, or the industry insider addressing an outsider.

Of course, a few knowledgeable and expert communicators avoid the curse of knowledge with apparent ease, but let's consider them outliers and confess that the rest of us struggle with it. The greater your knowledge, the stronger the curse.

Nonfiction writers confront this problem in many phases of the work. For example, we cannot proofread our own work effectively because we already "know" what's on the page. We use terminology that readers don't know because it is habitual to us.

You can defeat the curse of knowledge during later phases of the work by enlisting others for editing and proofreading. But you must avoid the curse earlier still, when deciding what to cover and how to approach it. Get outside your own head.

Go Wide or Go Deep

Before you write a single word, you face a fundamental decision about exactly what you want and need to cover. Answer these three questions.

1. Breadth: Will you cover a single issue or a wide range of topics?
2. Depth: Should you dive into details? How many are necessary?
3. Background: How much does the reader already know, and how much will you need to backfill?

These decisions depend almost entirely on your readers. For a distinct, well-defined audience, you may be able to cover a wider range of concepts related to your topic. When addressing a general audience, you may choose to focus on the most important things, and avoid excessive detail.

The final form also matters. A book gives you more room to roam; readers expect a greater breadth or depth of coverage.

If you are expert in a topic, you may choose to cover it in great detail. For example, masterful biographers like Doris Kearns Goodwin and Walter Isaacson do deep dives into their subjects' lives, creating works that span several hundred pages. If that's your approach, you will need to dedicate time and effort to maintaining the reader's interest. The depth of a treatment can narrow the potential audience of readers.

For some books, *breadth* is part of the essential value, as in Neil deGrasse Tyson's *Astrophysics for People in a Hurry*.

As the title promises, it describes a massive topic in a slim volume. Tyson went wide, not deep. Writing about complex topics effectively at this level is a rare skill. Tyson deploys analogies with care, frames the content in a human context, and shares his personal enthusiasm and sense of wonder to guide the reader through the universe. (These methods feature in upcoming chapters.) The book is a masterful example of writing about a complex and abstract topic.

There's no easy answer to the question of how broad or deep your treatment should be. It depends on your purposes and the needs of your audience.

Self-indulgent writers include everything they feel like covering. Thoughtful writers who seek to be understood focus on fit and purpose. Sometimes you have to let things go or put them aside for another project. Focus on serving your reader.

Simplicity vs. Oversimplification

Designers, businesspeople, and others often refer to of the KISS principle, which is an acronym for Keep It Simple, Stupid.

As a design philosophy, Keep It Simple, Stupid makes sense. Don't create systems that are more complex than necessary. However, people mistakenly apply the KISS mantra as a filter in other fields, including political messaging, sales materials, and descriptions of technology.

Simplicity isn't always the answer. The KISS mantra can become a convenient excuse for hiding complexity that you would rather people not see, such as:

- Removing transparency from investments, because investors don't need to know the possible risks
- Not disclosing details of policies because voters won't bother with the fine print
- Not communicating to patients the complete range of treatment options available or the potential risks of a recommended course of action, for fear of delaying the preferred course of treatment.

Taken to the extreme, the KISS mantra shields us from the complexity that we *should* understand.

Certain readers crave simplistic explanations or easy answers that spare them the cognitive work of understanding things that don't hold their interest. Others, however, may suspect that you're hiding important details or talking down to them.

When explaining complicated topics, beware of the boundary between simplicity and oversimplification.

We *want* to believe that the world is simple enough for us to understand. We like to think that we don't need layers of experts arbitrating between reality and ourselves, but when we ignore the true complexity of situations, bad things can happen.

News sources pander to the narratives people *want* to hear rather than the grittier realities of the world. So-called *fake news* flourishes because the truth is often nuanced and difficult. Albert Einstein once said, "Make it as simple as possible, but no simpler." (Full disclosure of annoying details: There's debate about whether Einstein said that, or if it's a paraphrase of something else.) The advice applies well for those of us writing about complicated topics. Get to the important points. Don't lead with the gnarly details, but don't hide them, either.

When writers make things seem too simple, even with the best intentions, they can inadvertently mislead readers.

Sabine Hossenfelder has heard some pretty wild theories about physics—hypotheses that she believes arise from the oversimplification of scientific topics for the general public. Hossenfelder is a theoretical physicist at the Frankfurt Institute for Advanced Studies, and writes about physics for publications like *Forbes* and *Scientific American*. She is also author of the book *Lost in Math: How Beauty Leads Physics Astray*.

Her insight into the dangers of oversimplification, however, arises from years spent running a "Talk to a Scientist" consulting service, which she started as a graduate student and still maintains today on her blog, *BackReaction*. For a small fee, members of the public can pose questions about physics, neuroscience, geology, and other topics, or submit their own ideas about physics. Those theories are creative, interesting, and often not grounded in scientific reality.

She blames this, in part, on the tendency of journalists covering the field to simplify the message so much that they mislead readers.

In describing the experience of running the physics help line, she reports, "The most important lesson I've learned is that journalists are so successful at making physics *seem* not so complicated that many readers come away with the impression that they can easily do it themselves. How can we blame them for not knowing what it takes *if we never tell them?*"[6]

Methods for Writers:
Deciding What to Include

Deciding what to cover and what to leave out challenges everyone. Writers, speaking coaches, and others share their advice about striking the right balance.

Get guidance from outsiders

When you're an insider in an industry, seek advice from those who are outsiders. Just make sure you find the right people to ask.

Linda Popky could be considered a Silicon Valley insider. She was named a Top 100 Women of Influence by the *Silicon Valley/San Jose Business Journal*, and works with tech companies as the founder and president of Leverage2Market® Associates. She's also the author of the book *Marketing Above the Noise: Achieve Strategic Advantage with Marketing That Matters.*

When writing about topics in which she has expertise, Popky takes care to counteract her insider status. "There are two dangers to knowing your subject matter well. First, you think everyone else knows it already, and as a result, no one understands what you write. Or, you think that *nobody* knows this stuff, and you go into excruciating detail."

She handles the situation by finding other people to give her an outsider's perspective. The key, says Popky, is getting feedback from the *right* individuals. "You need people who understand the audience and provide the right level of feedback at the right time. Find individuals who can express themselves and identify when something doesn't work for them. They need the honesty to say if something is confusing."

Identify your key points

When writing a relatively short article or blog post, you want to get your ideas across quickly and efficiently, before you lose the reader's attention. Public speakers face the same issue. So, for advice in this area, I turned to my friends Karen Catlin and Poornima Vijayashanker, co-authors of the book *Present! A Techie's Guide to Public Speaking.* These two women coach and train budding public speakers in the technology sector and beyond.

Says Catlin, "Engineers are so detail oriented. We feel like we need to explain *everything*. And we're logical. So the easiest piece of advice I give my coaching clients is this: If the audience will only remember two to three things from your talk, what would they be? Once you know those points, underline and repeat them."

Note that Catlin uses the word *underline* metaphorically. In speaking, you might underline a point by repeating it with a variation in phrasing or intonation. The chapter on repetition offers more advice for writers. In writing for print, please don't underline your key points. Let the words do that magic instead.

Don't cut—relocate

The average person is loss averse. Behavioral economists assert that we feel losses roughly twice as intensely as we do gains, which leads investors and gamblers to make irrational decisions.

Loss aversion also afflicts us when writing. The more time and effort we have invested in the words, the harder it is to cut them. That's a problem, because the most valuable editing tool is often the Delete key. Most experts want to share too much about the subject they love—more than the reader needs.

Cutting your hard work is painful, so reframe the way you think about paring down content. Instead of deleting sections, relocate them.

When editing my book manuscripts, I create a companion file called "Stuff that needs a new home." Title yours whatever you want. When you decide that certain content doesn't serve the reader's interest or interrupts the flow, relocate it to this file. Now you've got a rich source of material for other purposes, such as blog posts, articles, examples, speeches, or lessons.

Even if you never end up using the words in this file, having a home for unwanted text reduces the pain of deleting.

Rules to remember

- Decide what you are going to cover, and to what level of detail, based on the needs of the target audience rather than what you want to say.

- In general, increasing the depth of your coverage of a topic will decrease the reach of the audience, as fewer people are willing to dive deep into the weeds with you.

4

WHAT DO THEY ALREADY KNOW?

Why we think we know more than we do
How to address the knowledge illusion
The many types of misinformation

Imagine you're building a home on an empty lot. You are both architect and contractor. You've got the blueprints and plans for construction, but first, you have to survey the lot.

Is the lot cleared, graded, and ready to build on? Is it free of trash and debris? Maybe there's a garden shed to demolish, or a stand of mature trees to protect and preserve. If you're lucky, the utility lines are in place, plans approved, and foundation poured, saving you time.

As a writer, you face a similar situation building an edifice of understanding in the reader's brain. Before you begin the work, do a site survey of your audience's understanding of the topic. Make your best guesses for the following questions:

- What do the readers already know that is correct?

- What do they *imagine* they know about the topic?

- What do they believe that is wrong or incomplete?

Of course, the more you know and speak with your target audience, the easier it will be for you to answer these questions. If you don't address imagined knowledge and misinformation, you can lose the battle for the reader's attention and understanding before you begin.

We Think We Know More Than We Do

You know how a flush toilet works, right? How much do you *really* know, though, about why it flushes when you press the handle?

I know how to jiggle the handle if the seal isn't tight on the thingy in the tank. (The term *flapper valve* springs to mind.) But how does pushing that handle make the water flush, and how would I explain that function? If I had to teach someone else, let's just say that my sense of expertise would go right down the drain.

There's no way that we could understand a fraction of the technologies we use daily and still have time for a normal life. Every day I rely on the expertise of engineers, scientists, physicians, house builders, traffic engineers, and many more. Yet—and here's the rub—I feel pretty competent. I imagine that I know more than I do.

That's the essence of the issue that cognitive scientists Steven Sloman and Philip Fernbach describe in their book *The Knowledge Illusion: Why We Never Think Alone*. They write about a division of cognitive labor that is part of modern life. We cannot possibly know everything we need to know, so we rely on other experts to understand things for us. However, we unconsciously claim ownership of expertise that doesn't live in our own heads. We get so used to outside help that we don't see the boundaries of our understanding. As Sloman and Fernbach report, we rely on a *community of knowledge*. In their view:

> Individual knowledge is remarkably shallow, only scratching the surface of the true complexity of the world, and yet we often don't realize how little we understand.

The knowledge illusion isn't a bad thing. In a complex world, an unfounded sense of competence can be reassuring. My faith in my plumbing expertise helps me remain sane. Write Fernbach and Sloman, "We tolerate complexity by failing to understand it. That's the illusion of understanding."

I'm not alone in my unfounded sense of technical competence. The psychologists Leonid Rozenblit and Frank Keil[7] asked people to rate their understanding of common devices like zippers, cylinder locks, piano keys, and, of course, flush toilets. They devised a simple experiment:

1. On a scale of one to seven, subjects rated how well they understood the device.
2. Next, they were asked to write a detailed explanation of how the device worked.
3. After attempting the explanation, subjects once again rated their understanding.

As soon as people had to describe exactly how things worked, they downgraded their assessments of their own expertise. Rozenblit and Keil refer to this tendency as *the illusion of explanatory depth*. It explains a lot.

When we attempt to explain a concept, we run into the limits of our understanding. That's why teaching or writing about a topic makes us smarter about it.

When writing to explain, you may need to navigate the reader's illusion that they already know enough about the topic. Unlike these researchers, you cannot ask your readers to first write out a detailed explanation. You'll have to work around their illusion of knowledge, perhaps by appealing to their curiosity. (See Chapter 6.)

And while we rely on the broader community of knowledge to help us navigate a complex world, we're not always discriminating about our sources. As a result, we accumulate a lot of misinformation.

Misinformation: Lies and BS

Consider the numerous urban legends that persist to this day, despite constant debunking. Modern folklore is rife with stories of alligators in the sewers of New York City, stolen kidneys, and countless ghost stories. Some tales amuse while others frighten, propagating unfounded anxiety.

These legends spread and persist because they combine emotional context (often fear) with effective storytelling. (Chapter 9 describes the power of storytelling for getting your message across.)

Urban legends are not the only misinformation that plagues the modern world.

Individuals and institutions may knowingly propagate misinformation to manipulate public beliefs or to disguise their own behavior. Political campaigns have been known to deploy false stories to influence voters. The tobacco industry for years denied or marginalized science about the addictive qualities of smoking. Social media networks like Facebook have made it easier than ever for these stories to spread with the patina of truth and social proof, but misinformation has been around as long as people have communicated.

The Internet puts a world of data at our fingertips and in our phones, and not all of that data is trustworthy. We are quick to accept information as truth when it's presented online, without examining the motives or authority of the source. We are easily snookered by misleading graphics or cherry-picked data.

Complex topics are fertile ground for the weeds of misinformation. Consider a wondrously complicated event, like the moon landing. Against that backdrop, place a single observation, like the fact that NASA lost the tapes of the high-quality video feed of the first lunar landing, or that the moon seems so very far away. Put them together and you've got the origins of a longstanding conspiracy theory about faked moon landings. We are not comfortable with uncertainty and complexity, and sometimes would rather believe a simple idea that we can understand.

In his marvelous book *A Field Guide to Lies*, the neuroscientist Daniel Levitin writes:[8]

> It's important to accept that in complex events, not everything is explainable, because not everything was observed or reported.

Put this understanding of human cognitive foibles into the hands of entities that want to control our beliefs, and misinformation can take a dark turn into destructive rumor, political mudslinging, and intentional manipulation.

Liars and deceivers are not the only threat to our understanding. Some individuals spread opinions without *any* regard to veracity. In his scholarly essay *On Bullshit*, philosopher Harry Frankfurt differentiates between deliberately misleading another person about a topic and simply talking smoothly without regard to the facts. Bullshitters, according to Frankfurt, misrepresent *themselves*. They don't generally care about the truth or falsehood of their statements. Writes Frankfurt, "Bullshit is a greater enemy of the truth than lies are."[9]

Whether you're confronting actively disseminated doubt and misinformation or the product of loosely regulated thought and looser ethics, the result is the same. You need to deconstruct a belief that has already taken hold in the reader's head.

You cannot simply show up with a verbal wrecking ball, saying "trust me."

You'll need to earn trust and lead people to a different perspective, using the strategies in the latter two parts of this book.

Methods for Writers:
Surveying Existing Knowledge

To determine what your readers know, get to know your readers. When possible, converse with them in person. If your audience is too broad to survey, here are a few strategies you might use to scope out the extent of misinformation you may face.

Check social media

Because misinformation often proliferates on social media, the online world is a great place to survey people's opinions. You'll have to reach beyond your own networks, searching Twitter, if you dare, or conversations in Facebook groups or other places.

FactCheck.Org is one of several organizations now working with Facebook to root out fake news, and a good place to find trending stories. Snopes.com highlights myths and memes that need debunking.

Let Google help you

As the world's largest search engine, Google offers a portal into global searches through its autocomplete feature. Start a typing a question about your topic and see the suggested autocomplete searches. For example, typing "How the moon landing" in Google displays a number of suggested searches, including:

How the moon landing *changed technology*
How the moon landing *changed history*
How the moon landing *worked*

How the moon landing *was filmed*
How the moon landing *was faked*

That last one directed me to a Wikipedia page about the conspiracy theories. Its presence indicates that enough people question the moon landing to register in Google's search algorithms. What other unexpected questions might your readers have?

Writing Advice from a
Cognitive Scientist

Name: Dr. Steven Sloman

Experience: Professor of cognitive, linguistic, and psychological sciences at Brown University, co-author of *The Knowledge Illusion*, and Editor-in-Chief of the journal *Cognition*.

Special Skills: Explaining cognitive science to students, colleagues, and the general public

---

Dr. Steven Sloman teaches psychology to college students, contributes to and edits academic journals, and writes for the general public. Because he's an expert on the knowledge illusion, I couldn't resist asking him for writing advice.

Depth of detail

When it comes to determining how much detail to include, Sloman attempts to meet the needs of diverse subsets of his reading audience. "I've come to appreciate that in general, many readers don't want much detail. The critical thing with writing is to understand your reader. Many people prefer a shallow level of understanding."

Given this challenge, he chooses a "divide and conquer" approach to satisfying his readers. "You have to keep one group interested, while also satisfying the more reflective and detail-oriented readers. I try to appeal to both groups. First, I present a concept in a skeletal way, so the people who only want a high-level understanding get what they need. Then I describe the ideas in more detail for the second group, and the first group passes their eyes over it, feeling like they understand."

Yes, it's fitting that the author of *The Knowledge Illusion* knows he has to address that mental state in his own readers.

When academics write books for the general public, they sometimes overload the work with supporting evidence and citations. Sloman and his co-author, Fernbach, have resisted that temptation in their work. "That's what endnotes are for," comments Sloman.

Supplementing theory with story

Using story is an important part of writing about abstract topics. Sloman reports, "We spent a lot of time thinking carefully about which were the right stories to tell. We were very selective. There's a danger that when you rely on stories, you ignore statistics. I like to buttress the story with data. The fact that you're telling the story doesn't mean that you can't also offer a little science. Evidence and storytelling are separate but both necessary."

Combatting misinformation and beliefs

How should writers address readers who may suffer from the knowledge illusion, overestimating their existing understanding of the topic? Sloman and Fernbach warn against attempting to abruptly shatter people's illusions. Telling people that they're wrong is a great way to antagonize them.

When those illusions are based on underlying beliefs, getting past them can be more problematic. So I asked

Sloman for his advice. His response: "First, recognize the range of values out there, so the readers feel that their views have been acknowledged. If you're talking about abortion, for example, start with 'some people feel that abortion is murder and others that it represents an individual's personal choices.' Lay out the range of values first, then you can get into the topic without the reader feeling ignored or marginalized."

Second, Sloman suggests that writers focus the discussion on causes and consequences instead of values. "I take the distinction between sacred values and causal, explanatory thinking very seriously. Sacred values get passed down through the community. You can deal with sensitive issues effectively by making the discourse about causal relationships and consequences rather than sacred values and preferences."

Ultimately, reader response depends on their interpretation of your intentions in writing. "I think the critical variable, certainly for political or hot-button issues, is what you feel about the *intent* of the person giving you the information. Understanding writing and language is all about understanding intention."

One more thing: Be concise

This last bit of advice on writing from Sloman may be my favorite: "The number one attribute of good writers is being willing to delete."

5

THE TOUGH AUDIENCE

What "need for closure" does to audience receptivity
What to do when you run into self-sealing logic
Understanding your reader's moral taste buds

In April 2017, Chicago police forcibly dragged a passenger (a doctor, no less) from an overbooked aircraft when he refused to give up his seat. Fellow passengers caught and shared the violent scene on video.

The incident turned into an epic public relations failure for United Airlines when CEO Oscar Munoz weighed in. He aggravated the brand's situation through his choice of words in his first public response: "I apologize for having to *re-accommodate* these customers." (Italics are mine.)

The juxtaposition of the cold, corporate-speak word (re-accommodate) with images of the bloodied passenger was simply too powerful to ignore. The apology sounded like the embodiment of a heartless corporation, and Twitter blew up, seizing on the disparity between the words and the reality of the video.

When you ignore the audience context, you can lose control of the narrative. Munoz clearly understood that he was treading into a sensitive area. He may have chosen the word re-accommodate intentionally to create distance from the reality. Or, maybe it was the curse of knowledge in action—perhaps *re-accommodation* is an industry-standard term for what airlines do when flights are oversold. Either way, it didn't land well on an audience of people primed with violent video images. The words didn't match the context.

Munoz was writing for a tough audience, already offended. What's your audience primed to feel about your topic?

Reader Resistance

In most situations, your reading audience will consist of people who are friendly or neutral to your topic, if inattentive. Yet sometimes you need to reach readers who resist your message, for whatever reasons.

Succeeding with a tough audience isn't easy. Your success rate will never reach 100 percent. If you don't acknowledge the situation before you set out, however, you may lose more people than you reach.

You may not realize that your readers aren't receptive. Most of us have learned from experience which topics set off an emotional response in the people around us, but don't know how the larger world feels. We invite criticism and censure if we don't think through the context of our readers.

Even if your target audience is receptive, other people may not be predisposed to react well to your writing. To extend your reach, consider how to approach the tough audience.

Let's look at three types of potential resistance to your topic:

1. People who have already made up their minds and resist changing them
2. People who simply don't want to hear about what you're writing because they feel threatened by it at some level
3. Readers with deeply held beliefs that are in conflict with your ideas

The Made-Up Mind

If you're writing about topics with a great deal of ambiguity, be prepared to encounter the already-made-up mind in your readers.

The world is filled with complicated, ambiguous situations. It may take a while for the evidence to come in, or for a situation to clarify. During that transitional time, we either accept uncertainty or make provisional decisions.

Some people find ambiguity inherently painful or difficult to handle, and seize on a quick decision.

According to psychologist Arie Kruglanski, people exhibit different levels of a *need for closure* as a personality trait. Individual levels vary; you can take a quiz on Kruglanski's website to see where you land on his Need For Closure Scale.[10]

People with a strong need for closure tend to make decisions more quickly in uncertain situations. Having made a decision, they stick to it with more tenacity. And that tendency can lead them into trouble.

Imagine that you are asked to identify an ambiguous image that could be either a cat or a dog, depending on how you interpret it. There's no clear "right" answer. *You* see a dog, and make your choice.

Then, the image starts to shift, slowly and inevitably, into something that looks remarkably like a cat. It practically meows at you. At some point, you change your answer. "All right, that's a cat."

How long does it take you to *see* the cat as the image shifts? If you have a strong personal need for closure, then it will be difficult for you to detect the emerging cat. You continue to perceive the dog, even as the visual evidence points clearly toward the cat.

The cat/dog story comes from research conducted by Else Frenkel-Brunswik, whose work I only recently discovered. Having fled the Nazi incursion in Austria in 1938, Frenkel-Brunswick took up a role as a professor of psychology at the University of California, Berkeley. In the late 1940s, she conducted research to explore variations in human behavior and personalities. The dog/cat image study revealed how ambiguity tolerance affects *perception*.[11] When people with a low tolerance for ambiguity are forced to make a decision in an uncertain situation, they stick to their perception doggedly. (I couldn't resist the pun.)

It's perception, not stubbornness.

Remember that the next time you write about a nuanced topic that is still in flux, or for which recent evidence contradicts previous beliefs. Your reader may not be able to see the same things you do in the research.

If they have a strong need for closure, then it's not enough to simply shout at them with evidence: "It's a *cat*!" You'll need to try another approach to dislodge their fixed perceptions. If you present them with evidence that contradicts their earlier decisions, they'll experience *cognitive dissonance*—the state of discomfort that arises when a person holds two contradictory beliefs. That cognitive discomfort might create a shift in perception, or it might cause the person to dig in further and block out your words.

Remember that a straightforward, evidence-based approach may not work when minds are already convinced.

The Things We Don't Want to Hear

Every time I read a study about the evils of sugar, I start skimming. I simply don't want to hear about them. Over time, these reports are getting through and I am cutting back on sugar intake—reluctantly. In contrast, I'm *all over* any research about antioxidants in dark chocolate. I can spot those headlines from a mile away.

We all maintain filters for the facts and data we are willing to absorb. Consciously or not, we disregard research and opinions that threaten our beliefs, behavior, or chocolate consumption.

Resistance may be a simple case of denial. We don't want to think about these difficult situations, and hope that they will simply go away. Sometimes we know, deep down, that we should be paying attention.

The speaker of unwelcome truths—that's a role that Michele Wucker has willingly taken on with her book *The Gray Rhino: How to Recognize and Act on the Obvious Dangers We Ignore*. As a Guggenheim Fellow and a 2009 Young Global Leader of the World Economic Forum, Wucker has a track record of researching, writing, and speaking about the truths we need to heed.

The gray rhino is Wucker's metaphor for those obvious, high-probability problems that we choose not to think about. On an individual basis, ignoring our gray rhinos can be hazardous, such as when people in the path of a hurricane disregard evacuation orders, or heart-attack survivors neglect to make lifestyle changes. Entire societies ignore these risks as well, including problems like financial bubbles, growing inequalities, and climate change. According to Wucker:[12]

> A Gray Rhino is a highly probably, high-impact threat: something we ought to see coming like a two-ton rhinoceros aiming its horn in our direction and preparing to charge. Like its cousin, the Elephant in the Room, a Gray Rhino is something we ought to be able to see clearly by virtue of its size... To the contrary, the vary obviousness of these pachyderms is part of what makes us so bad at responding to them. We consistently fail to recognize the obvious, and so prevent highly probably high-impact crises: the ones we have the power to do something about.

If you're writing about a well-known risk, recognize the strength of any potential denial you might face. Find creative and constructive ways to invite the reader to contemplate topics they would rather ignore. Pay particular attention to upcoming chapters on analogies and storytelling, methods that can help you present obvious risks in a fresh light.

Wading into Deeper Values

Galileo is known today not only for his astronomical discoveries, but also for his battle with the Catholic Church over the issue of whether the Earth revolves around the sun. His story serves as a classic example of science versus religion, reason versus belief. At the core, Galileo and the Church argued about *different* things, so found no common ground. We hear echoes of this conflict today in issues such as climate change, vaccines, and evolution.

When your topic area impinges on your readers' moral or ethical beliefs, reason and evidence won't suffice.

When Galileo published his "Dialogue on the Two World Systems" in 1632, he knew *exactly* what he was doing. Galileo's society operated with clearly defined and codified values. He understood that he was launching a written grenade at the Pope, and did it anyway.

Modern-day writers may not realize when they trespass on deeply held beliefs. Our cultures are varied and heterogeneous. We don't always understand each other, and that leads to acrimonious disagreements. We unintentionally step on each other's beliefs all the time, often without being aware of the pain we are inflicting. As writers, we might alienate a reader with ideas that threaten loyalty to existing institutions, or that offend a sense of sanctity.

We are surprised when our rational, logical words create a storm of emotional response.

When writing to explain or convince people, recognize if you're not dealing in the realm of reason alone, but with emotional and moral concerns. The clearest explanations rarely make a dent in core beliefs and fundamental values.

As a management consultant and founder of the design consultancy XPLANE, Dave Gray works with major corporations to create and implement strategies for change. In his book *Liminal Thinking: Create the Change You Want by Changing the Way You Think*, he writes:

> Beliefs are unconsciously defended by a bubble of self-sealing logic, which maintains them even when they are invalid, to protect personal identity and self-worth.

The phrase *self-sealing logic* reminds me of run-flat tires, which let you keep driving when they get a puncture. They don't deflate, but you do need to replace them before long. Similarly, deeply held beliefs resist attempts to poke holes in their logic or consistency. Only in the case of beliefs, people can keep using them for a long time after they start springing leaks.

Your beliefs originate from many sources: family, religious or social institutions, personal observation, popular culture, the media, and more. They are not entirely shaped by rationality. They seem obvious to you, and thus are hard to detect.

We don't cling to all of our beliefs. Unimportant ones can be replaced on the basis of fresh evidence or shifting cultural norms. You *can* wear white after Labor Day? Cool!

Others invoke a stronger innate sense of right and wrong, and that's where things get interesting. Your ethical foundations may not match those of your readers. Actions that appear acceptable to you may seem reprehensible to others, or vice versa. When we encounter those situations, our words are likely to land on hostile soil, unless we prepare the ground ahead of time.

While it's impossible to survey all your readers' beliefs, you can start by assessing their overall moral beliefs and inclinations.

The Moral Taste Buds

In his book *The Righteous Mind*, social psychologist Jonathan Haidt describes six "foundations" of moral feeling and thought, which are shared between different people and cultures in different doses, and consist of:

1. Care/Harm (Does this harm someone?)
2. Fairness/Cheating (Is someone taking unfair advantage?)
3. Loyalty/Betrayal (Is this disloyal, unpatriotic, etc.?)
4. Authority/Subversion (Is this disrespectful?)
5. Sanctity/Degradation (Does this violate a deep inner sense of human dignity?)
6. Liberty/Oppression (Does this impede my freedom or rights?)

Haidt compares these values to taste buds. People have varying sensitivities to tastes, and the cuisines of various cultures stimulate those taste buds in different combinations. You may not like spicy food yourself, but you realize that billions of people around the world do.

The same is true with these ethical foundations. When people make moral judgments about a situation, they deploy a combination of these foundational issues.

Haidt suggests that many political divides result from mismatched moral foundations. Some people care primarily about care/harm or fairness/cheating, while others call on more of the foundations, including loyalty, respect, and sanctity. Physiological sources can affect these moral foundations as well. Having a strong, easily activated sense of disgust may predispose people to value sanctity and avoid things that seem abhorrent. You cannot simply reason away a reader's deeper beliefs. Haidt writes:[13]

> People sometimes have gut feelings—particularly about disgust and disrespect—that can drive their reasoning. Moral reasoning is sometimes a post hoc fabrication.

Given those different foundations, people will always disagree about what's right.

Society is best served when opposing sides collaborate and balance each other out. We can do that only if we listen to each other and interact with civility. Blindness to the other side's beliefs deepens our divides.

Methods for Writers
Connecting with People Across Beliefs

Writing about challenging or values-based topics requires a deft touch. Later chapters will discuss specific methods for addressing a difficult audience, such as storytelling and imagery.

You won't win over everyone. Perhaps you'll reach a few people outside your own sphere of followers or like-minded individuals. Maybe you'll reach a few *hundred*, or more. Start by setting realistic expectations.

There's no single formula for changing the beliefs of your readers—and that's a good thing. That doesn't mean you shouldn't try.

What *not* to do

Let's start with the easy part: what *doesn't* work. When writing about something that challenges or threatens a reader's fundamental beliefs, these strategies won't work:

Data, data, and more data. If you have an analytic bent, you may feel that you can change minds by providing more and better data. However, data alone rarely makes a lasting impression for people who are emotionally engaged with the subject. Answering emotion with data is like speaking to someone in a language they do not know. You won't reach agreement.

Remember the research about people who had a strong need for closure? They could stare at a picture of a cat and tell you it was a dog, if they had decided this was the case when the picture was less clear.

Or, remember Dave Gray's analogy of self-sealing belief systems? According to Gray, "If you give people facts without a story, they will explain it within their existing belief system."

Lecturing. Your perspective may be obvious to you, but not to your entire audience. When you fail to acknowledge other possible points of view, you risk disrespecting readers who don't agree with you. Beware of condescension and telling people how to think. Instead, help the reader see through another's eyes.

Insisting on being right. If you worry about defending the correctness of your opinions, then you may be focusing on *yourself* instead of the thoughts and ideas in the reader's head. To change someone's mind, guide them as they draw their own conclusions.

OK, that's what you should avoid. With that behind us, let's move on to methods you can deploy when writing for a difficult audience.

Survey your own beliefs and emotions

Before you can effectively reach people with different beliefs, first you must understand your own.

Which of the "moral taste buds" are strongest for you? You can assess your personal stance by taking the Moral Foundations survey at YourMorals.Org, where Haidt and colleagues continue to gather data.

Whatever you are writing about, stop first to consider what you may be taking for granted.

In his book *Liminal Thinking*, Dave Gray argues that we must cross the thresholds of our own belief systems to enter those of others. He advises that we should learn to understand the underlying emotions of our own opinions.

I asked him for his advice for writers in this situation, and this is what he offered: "I recommend that you learn to access your emotional state, especially as you react to new information or other people's ideas. Are you feeling curiosity or a more negative emotion, like fear, anger, or anxiety? If you have a strong emotional reaction to a concept, it's very likely you are having that feeling because the new information somehow threatens a belief that you hold. Ask yourself why you are feeling this way."

Emotional self-awareness, then, is the first part of the battle. Once we realize that we're in this territory, how does that influence our writing? We cannot ignore the emotional component; it must coexist with reason.

Says Gray, "You may want to bifurcate yourself into two personalities—the writer and the editor. The writer can be driven by strong emotion but the editor should keep a cool head and focus on triangulation. Ask yourself: Who agrees with these points? Who is likely to disagree? Who will be threatened by this?"

Fortified with a better understanding of your own biases, you're ready to try to cross the divide.

Reframe the values

Understand and appeal to the various ethical foundations (moral taste buds) of your readers. Anchor the discussion around the beliefs that are important to your audience. If you are hoping to reach a socially conservative readership, think about ways to address concerns of loyalty or sanctity.

For example, environmental issues can appeal to multiple moral foundations. The now-famous images of suffering polar bears trigger to the care/harm foundation, but there are many others. Do we have a sacred obligation to be caretakers of the planet? Do we demonstrate loyalty to the community and the next generation by taking a long view? Is it fair for one group to consume finite shared resources or take actions that affect impoverished countries around the globe?

Experiment with presenting your ideas in relation to different values, beyond the ones that seem obvious to you. Are there other angles to your subject that don't matter to you, but might resonate with resistant readers?

Once again, cognitive empathy is your ally. Revisit the methods in Chapter Two for ideas on finding your reader's perspective, and apply them to the people you feel will be most difficult to reach.

Rules to remember

Without having any easy answers for how to communicate with a tough audience, this is the best advice I can muster:

1. Understand the moral taste buds you may offend.
2. Observe your own beliefs.
3. Connect with your readers on levels beyond reason and data alone.
4. Don't expect complete success.

Writing Advice
from an Economist

Name: Michele Wucker

Experience: Author of *The Gray Rhino* and other books, Guggenheim Fellow, economist, general thought leader

Special Skills: Communicating about the risks people would rather ignore

---

As author of the book *The Gray Rhino*, Michele Wucker is accustomed to the challenges of writing and speaking about the risks we don't want to think about. I reached out to her for her advice on how to get past audience denial.

The first challenge is knowing when your topic is a gray rhino. Says Wucker, "If it makes you squirm even a bit, your topic is likely to be a gray rhino to someone. But you never know what will push people's buttons. We all see obvious challenges from different angles, so what one person sees as a threat might be an opportunity to another."

If you find yourself writing about this kind of topic, here's Wucker's advice on how to handle it.

Focus on the audience needs

She suggests that before you even start writing, frame your work in the terms of what the audience needs. "Who is your audience, and what do you want them to do or think differently because they read this piece? Knowing the answer to these questions helps you craft your writing to maximize its effectiveness. Once you have answered those questions, delve deeper: Are you writing from an angle that this audience finds important? Do you want them to change their minds, are you helping them to understand an issue, or both? Be sure that you're telling them something new—whether it's a new piece of information or a fresh way to look at something they think they know."

Test your message

With her focus on the audience needs, it's no surprise that Wucker tests her message extensively. She first used the gray rhino concept at a speech at the World Economic Forum Annual Meeting at Davos, Switzerland—an audience well schooled in the concept of risk. She also conducted roundtables with economists. Then she showed the work to people outside of the field of economics and policy, to test it with a broader audience.

Focus on the positive

When writing about obvious risk, it's easy and tempting to dwell on the downside, or attempt to spur action by highlighting the magnitude of the risk. This approach can backfire. Say Wucker, "Write to hope, not just to fear. There's a lot of contradictory research into what motivates people most: fear or optimism. But you don't want to put your readers into such a funk that they give up on the problem at hand, or worse, on finishing reading what you've written! Include ideas for solutions and stories of people who can inspire your readers through their work."

Watch your tone and style

She offered a number of guidelines for tone and style as well.

- Don't preach.

- Don't bombard people with facts, but do include enough facts, in context, that you have strong evidence to back up your point of view.

- Steer clear of anything that sounds like a personal attack; constructive criticism of behavior or outcomes is important and necessary, but the moment you sound like you're going after someone as a human being, you put your own credibility on the line.

- Don't use hot-button words that raise up reader defenses.

Don't expect to reach everyone

Finally, Wucker accepts that there will always be pushback when writing about this sort of topic. A few people tell her that her idea isn't counterintuitive *enough*. Others quip that if nothing is predictable, why try foreseeing anything? Occasionally, she encounters people surprised to find a woman writing about ideas in economics or finance.

It can take a tough skin to hunt the gray rhinos. But it's important work.

PART TWO

HOW TO EXPLAIN
ABSTRACT IDEAS

6

CURIOSITY IS YOUR ACCOMPLICE

Theories of curiosity as pain and pleasure
Why the beginning may be the most important thing you write
What clickbait headlines teach us about catching the reader's interest

In 2012, scientists at CERN's Large Hadron Collider announced they had observed a particle consistent with theories of the Higgs boson. The discovery reverberated through the mainstream press as well as the science journals. The international media faced a challenge nearly as daunting as that of observing the particle: finding a way to activate the general public's interest in a hard-to-comprehend discovery.

It's tough to get people curious about topics in which they have little background knowledge. Curiosity requires a degree of familiarity.

Journalists struggled to describe the importance of the discovery. Mainstream press focused on the human stories of individual physicists: the tension, the celebrations, and so on. Or they pulled out the "God particle" label to incite curiosity. God? In a particle?

Creative journalists reverted to colorful prose and metaphor, such as this one from a science article by Dennis Overbye in the *New York Times* on July 4, 2012:[14]

> Like Omar Sharif materializing out of the shimmering desert as a man on a camel in 'Lawrence of Arabia,' the elusive boson has been coming slowly into view since last winter, as the first signals of its existence grew until they practically jumped off the chart.

Does that capture your interest in a subatomic particle? If so, it's because these journalists are working hard to activate your innate curiosity.

The Science and Joys of Curiosity

Curiosity, as a cognitive state, is complicated.

Psychologist George Loewenstein defines human curiosity as a desire to fill an unmet need. In a 1994 article on the psychology of curiosity, Loewenstein proposed his *information gap* theory, in which curiosity is "a form of cognitively induced deprivation that arises from the perception of a gap in knowledge or understanding."[15]

In this light, curiosity is that itch you have to scratch. That makes sense, but it doesn't entirely match my experience. Any mystery reader or puzzle fan will tell you that confronting the unknown does not have to be uncomfortable. Many people find joy and satisfaction in solving puzzles or learning new things. I trust that you, as a reader of this book, find pleasure in discovering and exploring topics.

Psychologist Jordan Litman writes of *epistemic curiosity* as the positive experience of satisfying a desire, rather than scratching an uncomfortable itch. (*Epistemic* means 'relating to knowledge.') He divides this knowledge-loving curiosity into two types. One (I-type) is based on the intrinsic desire to learn, while the other (D-type) arises from satisfying an unmet need to eliminate uncertainty. Litman reframes the knowledge gap as something that is fun to bridge, rather than painful to experience.[16]

Whether pleasure or pain, curiosity clearly runs deep in our human nature. As a species, human beings have benefited significantly from our ability to learn, and curiosity spurs learning.

How can you activate your readers' curiosity?

If you want to appeal to the intrinsic desire to learn (Litman's I-type of curiosity), offer the promise of fresh information that the readers will enjoy acquiring. In marketing terms, *lead with the benefit.*

To appeal to Litman's D-type, deprivation-based curiosity, induce a knowledge gap: expose contradictions, paradoxes, or puzzles, or pose an intriguing question. Having activated the gap, make sure to fill it.

Don't make the gap too wide. Readers are willing to stay with you long enough to fill a short gap in their understanding. Presented with a yawning chasm, they may abandon you. In the book *Why: What Makes Us Curious,*

astrophysicist and author Mario Livio writes of finding a
sweet spot, a Goldilocks balance of things we know and do
not know:[17]

> We are not particularly interested in subjects
> about which we know almost everything or prac-
> tically nothing. We tend to be interested when we
> know quite a bit but feel that there is more to be
> learned.

As you determine how broad or deep to go in covering your topic, remember that you are doing a dance with
your readers' curiosity. Figure out how to connect with
what they know while engaging them with the unknown.
Anchor abstract or novel topics in familiar frameworks to
find a curiosity sweet spot.

The Role of Curiosity in Beginnings

Malcolm Gladwell's best-selling book *The Tipping Point*
opens with the detailed description of a village in Italy.
Rosa Parks refusing to give up her seat occupies the opening passage of Susan Cain's excellent work on introversion,
*Quiet: The Power of Introverts in a World That Can't Stop Talk-
ing*. Daniel Pink's 2018 book *When* launches with the
departure of the *Lusitania* ocean liner from New York
in 1915.

Of the nonfiction books intended for a general audience on my bookshelf, a large percentage begin with a
story that, at first glance, has *nothing* to do with the title of
the book. Yet I trust that the author will make the connection and I'm curious about what it will be.

We can learn from these expert explainers. Launching your book with the *Lusitania* may be a bold move, if you are superstitious. But while the ship sinks, the book takes off by linking the tragic scope of the story with the premise of the work: the importance of timing on human behavior.

Pink, Cain, Gladwell, and countless successful nonfiction authors understand that their first job is to catch the reader's attention. Without that interest, no amount of brilliant explaining will matter, because the reader won't be around to notice.

Your window of opportunity for earning attention is quite short; it lasts as long as the title of your piece and, if you're lucky, the opening lines. You may spend hours, days, months, or years tuning your arguments and building your expertise. Without an effective opening, all that work is for naught.

Marketing copywriters talk about the importance of having a *hook*, in everything from ad copy to blog posts. The hook entices the audience to click your link, pick up your book, or open your magazine article.

Yet even in the discipline of marketing, you'll hear different definitions of what makes an effective hook. One classic definition is a short sentence or tagline that describes the primary benefit, like the *New York Times* tagline: "All the News That's Fit to Print." Marketers also create headline hooks that appeal to curiosity or the fear of missing out: "You won't believe what happened next!"

The most effective hooks either pitch a powerful benefit or activate the reader's curiosity.

The chief objective of a title or an introduction is to find the intersection between the audience interest and what you want to communicate. Without an effective beginning, you may lose the reader altogether.

- Books connect with potential readers starting with the title and book description, and continuing into the introduction and first chapter.

- For a blog post, the starting promise may be expressed in the title and opening sentences.

- In an academic article or report, the title and the executive summary entice people to read further.

If you are creating narrative nonfiction, telling a story related to your content, remember that you don't have to open with the very beginning and proceed in chronological order. The middle of the story may make the most intriguing starting point.

If the target audience already knows something about your topic, then you have a rich variety of angles to consider for your opening. If not, find a relevant connection to their lives (a benefit) or a way to engage their curiosity.

Clickbait and Curiosity

We often direct our attention to things that are novel or unexpected, or conflicting information that we need to resolve. Headline writers exploit that tendency, creating a new writing genre of "clickbait" headlines.

A quick study of clickbait illustrates how marketers and others regularly exploit our curiosity: "This man opened the hood of his car, and you won't believe what happened next!" Or "Four ways you're losing money right now!"

Clickbait is manipulative and not sustainable. When you click through to the articles, the promised revelation rarely lives up to the hype.

If these headlines are so disappointing, why do they keep working? Why do you still feel the temptation to click on them? The proliferation of clickbait is a testament to the power of human curiosity. While I don't suggest you write cheesy and manipulative headlines, you can glean insight from the techniques of those who do.[18]

A few (real) BuzzFeed headlines demonstrate common themes:

- An incomplete story: *This girl matched on Tinder with an Olympic athlete and here's what happened next*

- An apparent conflict or surprise: *"O Canada" is your surprising new summer jam*

- Personal relevance: *What secret wish of yours is going to come true this year?*

If you're writing for people unfamiliar with your topic, with no apparent overlap between their interests and yours, these tactics hold vital clues for engaging the reader's curiosity. In other words, think like a clickbait writer, then dial it *way* back.

Methods for Writers:
Activating the Reader's Curiosity

Engaging the reader's curiosity "sweet spot" requires a balance of the known and unknown. If you are writing about an abstract and unfamiliar topic, find ways to link it to patterns or subjects familiar to the reader.

Remember the competing theories about curiosity; it can signal an information gap, or a fulfillment of purpose and acquisition of knowledge. If you want to activate the knowledge gap, take a page from the Buzzfeed headline writers and explore the following patterns:

- Novelty: things the reader has not yet heard or seen—including incomplete stories

- Unexpectedness: things that do not follow expected patterns or that conflict with existing evidence

- Personal relevance

The knowledge gap shouldn't be a chasm. For particularly knotty and complex subjects, consider breaking explanations into smaller leaps, then enticing the reader through each step.

To appeal to the reader's epistemic curiosity, or the joy of learning for its own sake, lead with the benefits of what the reader is going to learn. Start with telling them why they want to continue reading.

When it comes to appealing to the reader's curiosity, there's no better place to start than at the beginning—catching the reader's attention. Depending on what you're writing, you may have multiple starting points to work with. For most of us, the battle for the reader's attention is won or lost in the following two points: the title and the introduction.

Titles

Too often when picking a title, we try to encapsulate everything that follows. (I've done this myself.) But the most effective titles don't summarize the writing: they spark curiosity or hint at the benefits of reading.

Let's return to Neil DeGrasse Tyson, who writes about astrophysics for a general audience with great success. The title of his book *Death By Black Hole and Other Cosmic Quandaries* appeals to our curiosity (the knowledge gap) and certainly catches the attention of anyone who has ever watched a *Star Trek* episode: *What would death by black hole be like? Do tell.*

In contrast, *Astrophysics for People in a Hurry* presents the twofold promise of the book up front: it will be easy to read, and it won't take itself or its subject too seriously. The title leads with the benefit: easily accessible descriptions of astrophysics. It also invokes the "joy of learning" aspect of curiosity.

Introductions

Browse through the work of your favorite nonfiction authors and you'll find that they typically deploy one of two strategies in their introductions: leading with a benefit or appealing to curiosity.

You could choose other methods. You might decide to begin with a long discourse about why your topic matters, or the historical background for your subject. Take it from a former marketer—these approaches may alienate or bore many readers who would otherwise find your topic interesting, if you have a chance to reach them.

Find a good starting point, then bring the reader along with you.

Rules to remember

- Pay particular attention to the reader's curiosity when you craft introductions and titles.

- Lead with one of the two theories of curiosity: the benefit of learning something new, or the gap of what readers need to know.

- Find angles that are unexpected, apparently contradictory, or relevant to the readers' lives.

Writing Advice
from a Behavioral Designer

Name: Nir Eyal

Experience: Behavioral designer, best-selling author, tech company founder, consultant, and teacher

Special Skills: Understanding and explaining habit-forming behavior

---

When it comes to hooking your readers, who better to ask than Nir Eyal, the author of *Hooked: How to Build Habit-Forming Products?*

In his writing, Eyal dives into research spanning the fields of cognitive science, product design, and technology. In his blog *NirAndFar*, he explains these topics for the general, curious audience.

Finding his ideal readers

When I asked Eyal who he wrote for, his answer was *himself*. More specifically, "Both of my books have been based on personal questions that I wanted to answer. With *Hooked*, I got lucky, because lots of other people were interested in the topic. This is the opposite of how we design products."

In this case, personal curiosity led to the book. I can relate to that.

While it sounds self-serving, <u>focusing on his own needs helps Eyal empathize with the audience.</u> For example, he uses his own interest levels as a guidepost. "If I'm not curious about the topic, the reader won't be. If I ever feel that it's boring, I know that I'll lose the reader."

So, he writes for people who share his general sense of interest and curiosity. But he also works on their behalf. "I take complex ideas and save the reader thousands of hours reading journals and academic publications."

His commitment to reader needs shows up in many ways. For example, the posts on his blog include an estimated reading time metric. Is this based on deep research, I asked him? No. "I put it there because *I* want to know how long something is before I start reading." In short, he treats his readers the way that he, as a reader, hopes to be treated.

Behavioral design and writing

Eyal's basic model for designing habit formation includes four stages: the Trigger, the Action, the Variable Reward, and the Investment. (For more on this, read *Hooked*.) So, how does this map to writing?

Your title or introduction might serve as the *trigger*. The *action* you want the person to take is to read. The *investment* might happen when readers internalize your ideas. But according to Eyal, *variable rewards* are the key to keeping readers engaged.

"The research on variable rewards covers things like gambling and slot machines, but intermittent reinforcement for behavior happens everywhere. What makes for a good story is the same thing that keeps people at a blackjack table—mystery. I want the reader to have an unanswered question in their mind. If they don't, they won't keep reading. They need a constant itch to get to the end and discover the answer."

Meeting and satisfying the reader's curiosity is a form of variable reward, and it's what keeps people engaged.

Using pictures

Eyal's book uses a simple diagram, the Hook Model, displaying the four key phases of building habits. Says Eyal, "The other thing I strive for is to supplement a complicated idea with a model or picture. The Hooked loop is a picture you can digest and share easily."

According to Eyal, the act of drawing the diagram helps him focus on the essentials of the topic. "If you can't explain it simply, you don't understand it. Once you can visualize the idea, everything changes."

Deciding what to cover and what to leave out

For Eyal, the picture became a guide to deciding what belonged in the book. He used the discipline of creating an image to filter out the interesting but unnecessary or distracting research.

"There's so much I could have put in the book. When I drew the picture, with its four key elements, I knew what *shouldn't* go in the book. Cutting is always the most challenging part of writing. I can't tell you how many pages I cut from the drafts of my books. I spend so much time learning, and want to share it all. 'Look at this amazing stuff, let me lecture you on what I found.' That tends to be what I cut."

7

ABSTRACTIONS AND DETAILS

When abstract reasoning leads to cognitive load
How examples help us remember and understand abstractions
Why you should lead with the abstract, then get to the detail

A literate, informed citizen of the twenty-first century may need to understand or appreciate highly abstract concepts, such as:

- Subatomic particles and nanotechnologies too small to see

- Global trends too large to visualize

- Concepts like time, debt, and statistical probabilities that have no tangible form

- Abstract technical terms like *blockchain*, *the cloud*, and *the dark Internet*

We cannot see or touch these concepts. They exist entirely in the brain's higher-order, abstract thought processes.

Human beings are adept at abstraction. We see a variety of chairs and easily group them into categories: office chairs, furniture, things that have four legs, etc. But take care. Just because we're naturals at abstract reasoning doesn't mean that it's always easy to read and understand abstractions.

What's Going On in the Readers' Heads

Imagine that you could see the activity in the reader's brain when reading your explanation of an abstract topic. You are Superman, but instead of X-ray vision, you have functional magnetic resonance imaging (fMRI) vision. What would you see?

As the reader reads and interprets your words, the prefrontal cortex would be firing away behind the forehead. This part of the brain is responsible for—well, being responsible. It handles decision-making, social behavior, planning, and sticking to tasks like reading when we'd rather be doing something else. It's also where we manage the categorical thinking essential to working with abstract concepts.

The prefrontal cortex doesn't fully develop, on average, until around age twenty-five. That fact explains *so much* about teenagers and young adults.

Every abstract idea, theory, and concept you throw at the reader is fodder for the prefrontal cortex. Its capacity isn't infinite, and that same area is engaged in other pursuits while reading, like reigning in wandering attention and remembering to get to the office on time.

The amount of work going on is referred to as *cognitive load*. Depending on the reader's situation, you can overload the capacity of the prefrontal cortex to handle the work you're throwing at it. When that happens, something has to give. If you impose too much cognitive load on a reader, there's a good chance that their attention will wander. They may let their eyes skim over the words without comprehending. (We've all done that, right?) Or, they might simply put the reading down and walk away.

You cannot explain anything effectively to an overloaded reader.

Reducing Unnecessary Cognitive Load

If you want people to understand the essence of your explanation, clear away the small distractions and unnecessary load.

Much of this clearing happens in the revision and editing process. For example, readers use working memory to parse long, complex sentence structures including multiple dependent clauses. That's working memory squandered on interpreting your *sentences*, not the subject of the sentences.

You don't have to dumb down your work, but if your academic writing style involves a certain grammatical showmanship, reconsider your style when addressing a general audience. Readers who are already familiar with your topic have more brain cycles available for decoding your prose, *if* you want to put them through that. Adding grammatical complexity to subject complexity can overload the reader who is an outsider to your field. You will be less effective at explaining, or being understood.

You can also minimize the load by reducing the amount of abstract concepts that the reader has to deal with. Expendable abstractions usually include terminology and jargon—the words and phrases that are familiar to you, as an expert in your field, but may be foreign to the reader.

Writers who are experts become so accustomed to industry terms that they are like friends, as familiar as categories like *animals* or *furniture*. To a reader without that background, the words may seem alien.

Go through your work and differentiate between the following:

- *Necessary vocabulary*: those terms that are essential to the field or that save you, the writer, so much time in communicating that you want the reader to be comfortable with them

- *Unnecessary terminology*: words or phrases for which perfectly reasonable and accessible alternatives exist

If you're writing about collateralized debt obligations, you'll need to use the term, unless there's a synonym I don't know about. You can even abbreviate it to CDO. First, however, familiarize readers with both the term and the abbreviation, so they don't have to wrack their memories to decode it each time it appears.

Having cleared away unnecessary clutter, help readers navigate the abstractions of your writing. For that, you'll need to rely on finding the right balance of abstract and concrete, theory and detail.

Illustrating the Abstract with Concrete Examples

In our everyday lives, we constantly form working theories based on observations. Toddlers learn that when they pull the cat's tail, the cat scratches them. Beginning drivers learn how the rules of the road really work in their city through experience. Scientists use experiments to prove or disprove theories, again using detail to advance or eliminate a theory. All advanced learning is grounded in the interplay of abstraction and detail. So it follows that writing about these fields requires a similar balance.

When attempting to explain complicated topics, writers often fall into one of two traps.

The conclusion-only approach: Expert writers may remain entirely in the realm of the abstract while discussing their theories. Having worked so hard to master the abstractions, they want to show us what they know. This approach can be deadly boring for the readers, who must understand and accept the theory without the reinforcing details and observations.

The linear thinking approach: Other writers want to lead the reader carefully through the exact same set of observations and linear reasoning that they experienced in reaching their conclusion. While this may create an accurate, blow-by-blow representation of how they arrived at their opinions, it can be tedious for the reader to absorb. They may not come along for the ride.

Academic writing often uses both of these approaches. The executive summary of nearly any journal article spends all its time in the abstract, while the detailed methods section provides the blow-by-blow.

When writing for a general audience, try alternating between theory and example, abstraction and detail.

Concrete examples give readers a respite from juggling the concepts in their brains, particularly if the abstractions are unfamiliar to them. If you are writing about coniferous forests and then describe a specific forest of tall pine trees, the visual and tactile regions of the reader's brain will start firing. Add a quick mention of the fragrance and you've engaged another sensory system. Now the prefrontal cortex has company as it slogs through the content.

The right details make the work more interesting, support comprehension, and help the reader remember what you've written.

So details are important, but when and how should you use them? It depends on your purposes. If you're writing in hopes of *teaching* others about your subject, pay careful attention to the cadence of abstraction and detail.

According to John Medina, a molecular biologist and author of the best-selling *Brain Rules*, teachers shouldn't dive into details unless they have created the context for them. He writes:[19]

> If you want people to be able to pay attention, don't start with the details. Start with the key ideas and, in a hierarchical fashion, form the details

around these larger notions. Meaning before details.

Medina suggests that to improve learning, you should organize information in a logical format and present the theory first. He also recommends breaking lectures into ten-minute segments, each covering one core concept that can be explained within one minute. I can think of several classes I've taken that would have benefitted from this approach.

Clearly, listening to a college lecture isn't the same as reading. For example, in writing it's often productive to begin with an attention-grabbing, unexpected detail to arouse the reader's curiosity, as mentioned earlier, and then dive into the theory. But the general advice about combining theory and detail, in clear order, makes sense.

When Detail Is Data

Data is a special kind of concrete detail that both illustrates and supports theories.

Data may have a starring role in your writing. Remember this: When writing for a general audience, data is an *ingredient*, not the finished product of your writing.

Interpreting data requires a type of analytical thinking that many readers avoid when experiencing cognitive load. If you lead with data by itself, people might draw the wrong assumptions. Or, they may feel mistrustful of the data, if they suspect you're using dubious to shore up your arguments. As Mark Twain reportedly said, there are three types of lies: lies, damned lies, and statistics.

If you are accustomed to submitting to peer-reviewed academic journals, you may want to supply as much data as possible to reinforce your position. That instinct does *not* serve you well when writing for a general audience. If data doesn't advance the narrative or illustrate a relevant point, then it belongs in the endnotes, not the body of the text.

The more time you've spent gathering supporting data and research, the more tempted you are to flood the reader with that information. Depending on your audience, too much data may backfire. In the chapters that follow, we'll consider other ways to expand on the abstract, including analogies and stories.

Methods for Writers:
Working with Abstractions

If you write about abstract ideas, you'll need to find your own unique balance of detail, data, and theory—one that feels right to you and that works for your readers. Make sure the abstract concepts don't create barriers for readers unfamiliar with your field.

Eliminate the unnecessary

Thanks to the curse of knowledge, you may forget what it's like *not* to know and speak in the terminology of your field. The more familiar you become with these terms, the more they creep into your everyday vocabulary.

Notice the abstract terms in your writing. These might include terms or acronyms that are specific to your field alone. Print out your writing, pick up a highlighter, and mark as many as you can find.

Eliminate the ones that are not necessary.

Much academic writing is filled with the terms of the field. Outside the world of academia, this writing falls flat. If you're writing for the rest of us, remove the unnecessary jargon and replace it with ordinary, everyday words we can interpret easily. Remember, you want the reader to invest their cognitive load on understanding your topic, not decoding the words you use.

Unpack the unfamiliar

For those necessary abstractions, determine which ones might be unfamiliar to the reader. If you're not sure, ask someone who can put themselves in the shoes of the target audience. Make sure this person is not ashamed to say, "I don't know this" or "I had to stop and think about what this meant."

Some of these abstract concepts will be necessary. If you're talking about black holes, you'd better use that term, but define it first. Here's are a few guidelines for using industry-specific terminology that you deem necessary:

1. Define a term the first time it appears
2. Use the term in a context that reinforces the meaning the first few times
3. Occasionally sprinkle in specific examples to remind the reader

Even if you think most readers will have encountered the abstraction before, many won't mind a quick and painless refresher.

Add concrete examples and data

Because people cannot easily envision or manipulate unfamiliar abstractions in their heads, give them something they can hold on to: concrete examples, details, or data. While you might lead with an abstract idea (furniture), provide a solid, understandable detail (a desk chair). Adding sensory detail (a rickety black desk chair) gives their brains something to work with.

Writers who are expert explainers alternate between detail and theory, choosing the right details to support the ongoing discussion.

Tactics to try

- Alternate between the abstract and concrete details.

- For learning purposes, lead with the abstract (the theory), then introduce the detail. Otherwise, people often gloss over the detail, or may get distracted noticing extraneous patterns.

- Choose interesting or unusual details to capture the reader's interest, particularly if you're writing about topics that are foreign or difficult for the reader.

Writing Advice
from a Logical Reasoning Expert

Name: Ellen Cassidy
Experience: LSAT expert, instructor, and author
Special skills: Teaching logical reasoning and analytical thought

---

Ellen Cassidy *loves* logical thinking. She was admitted to Harvard Law School but had so much fun taking the LSAT, the standardized test for law school admission, that she changed her career course entirely. She started tutoring prospective law students in the logical reasoning part of the test. In doing so, she analyzed her own critical thinking, and created rules and practices to apply to the process.

Her excitement and love of the topic has led her to dedicate years to writing a guide teaching those skills, *The Loophole in LSAT Logical Reasoning*. So she seemed like the perfect person to interview on the topic of writing about abstractions.

Understanding her audience

Cassidy works with prospective test-takers every day, so she understands their perspective and the magnitude of her challenge. She accepts that her readers don't exactly approach the topic with a sense of glee or curiosity. They're not eager. Says Cassidy, "No one wants to read about logical reasoning. They *have* to. The LSAT is the big, scary monster they have to deal with. They are skeptical, and they are in a bad mood."

Lucky for them, then, that Cassidy's passion for the topic and commitment to her readers combine to make her a highly effective communicator. "I wanted to humanize something that can be really difficult and inaccessible. I want the readers to know that I'm on their side."

In taking on this challenge, she has created a book that defies the usual conventions of LSAT test prep.

Teaching the abstract through the details

Logical reasoning questions on the LSAT follow a general format: a short paragraph followed by a question. The paragraphs are often dry, complex, and difficult to understand. Instead of choosing similarly yawn-worthy topics, Cassidy teaches the readers about logical reasoning with nonsensical or absurd examples, such as pretzels that eat people, or microphones drinking coffee.

That nonsense is there for a sound reason. These examples counteract the urge to *guess* the answer based on prior subject knowledge, rather than logic. "People think they know stuff and will guess the answers on the test," she explains. "But that won't get you the correct answer. I have to build invisible fences so it's impossible to make those errors. When I use impossible, surreal examples, the readers only have the language of the example. There's a whole category of mistakes they cannot make."

More realistic questions appear once students master the abstract concept.

The power of the unexpected

These strange examples have another benefit: They surprise the reader. Remember that encountering the unexpected or novel sparks curiosity. Cassidy catches and sustains the readers' attention as they go through the difficult work of doing the exercises and mastering the underly-underlying logic.

Says Cassidy, "I know I am fighting Instagram. This is a book for people who would rather be on Instagram. I have to put a bit of what they like in there."

Writing voice

Cassidy's writing style is *not* the norm in the test prep industry. She begins the book with a dialogue between herself and the reader, invoking a sense of shared identity. She writes with humor and humility—topics coming up in Chapters 13 and 14.

This approach requires courage. "I had to learn not to be afraid to write in my own voice. I write with the reader in mind, and don't try to imitate every other book out there. My tutoring students love the style. I have no illusion that every person is going to love the style. That's OK. I'd rather be loved by a few."

She has received pushback on her humorous, informal style—not from students or readers, but from people familiar with traditional test preparation. She holds her ground. Says Cassidy, "People don't realize how hard it is to be funny and clever and unexpected. I would not cut those examples, no matter what."

8

EXPLANATORY ANALOGIES

Using an analogy as the foundation for your explanation
Why analogies are powerful for abstract ideas
Finding the right fit

Nonfiction authors stalk analogies the way big-game hunters track elusive prey. Nothing excites them as much as finding the perfect comparison to make their prose sparkle, their themes hang together, and the readers gasp, "Oh, I see!"

Analogies illuminate complicated topics by comparing them to objects we understand, experiences we have had, or situations we can imagine. Analogies are accelerants for the fire of understanding. (See what I did there?)

Watching an analogy unfold can be fun as well as edi-fying, satisfying a sense of curiosity. There's a reason that the "All the world's a stage" speech from Shakespeare's *As You Like It* is so well known. Having started with the metaphor of life as a play, Shakespeare (via the character Jacques) elaborates through the seven "acts" of man's life. The audience listens, reflects, and relates. (Bonus points to Shakespeare for getting it done in iambic pentameter.)

That fun evaporates quickly if the comparison doesn't quite work, or if we fundamentally don't understand it. Getting analogies right is tricky.

Analogies can serve many purposes in nonfiction writing.

One-time explanatory devices: You might use an analogy to explain a specific point or illustrate a set of relationships relative to your topic. In this situation, the comparison helps the reader comprehend a specific concept. Once the point is made, you can move on.

Foundational analogies: Writers often construct arguments, theories, or entire books around a metaphor or comparison. The analogy provides overarching structure for people to navigate during a prolonged explanation. It might help readers remember the key points. If you're going to stake your entire project on an analogy, though, you'd better find one that fits well.

Figures of speech: Writers often sprinkle metaphors and similes in their prose to make the writing interesting. Common figures of speech often embed images that we're not even aware of using.

We'll consider the power and uses of figurative language in more detail in Chapter 11. Now we'll explore the first two applications, using analogy to explain. Let's start by considering what happens in the reader's mind when analogy works.

The Cognitive Impact of Analogy

Analogies can activate the reader's curiosity as well as sensory processing and emotions. They are also exceptionally effective at explaining abstract ideas and relationships. When faced with abstract topics, analogies give our minds concrete ideas to work with. They are particularly effective for explaining relationships between abstract ideas or the behavior of unseen forces.

For example, the field of physics relies heavily on analogies to describe theoretical forces. String theory likens the interaction of unseen particles to the behavior of strings. The paradoxes of quantum mechanics come to life in a thought experiment involving a cat in a box (Shrödinger's cat).

People who write or speak about technology also compare the hidden aspects of technology to ordinary, everyday activities. Sarah Granger, a digital media entrepreneur, writer, and author of *The Digital Mystique*, relies on metaphors that connect the unseen world of technology with familiar objects.

If I were to write an article about a denial-of-service attack, which is a type of computer hacking, I might relate it to pouring so much coffee into a cup that the cup overflows. The coffee is the metaphor for the excessive messages or pings the hackers send to the server they want to reach. All that data coming at once overwhelms the server and it can't handle the load, and nothing else can get in. Service is denied. The coffee cup has to be cleaned up and emptied before it can be used again. Same with the server.

The familiar image (coffee and a cup) makes the unseen (Internet traffic) understandable.

The effectiveness of the analogy depends on two key factors: whether the reader is familiar with the subject of the comparison, and how well it fits the topic being explained.

Familiarity

Remember the curse of knowledge—the difficulty of remembering what other people *don't* know? It can get in our way when choosing an effective analogy.

If you're comparing **x** to **y**, what does the reader already know about **y**? If the image might puzzle a subset of readers, you'll need to explain it. If the analogy is critical to your explanation or if it serves as a structure for your piece of writing, provide in-depth background.

A foundational analogy doesn't have to be familiar to the audience at the start, because you can spend time elaborating on it. For example, in The *Black Swan: The Impact of the Highly Improbable*, essayist and author Nassim Taleb describes unexpected, unlikely risks as black swans. To make his case, he first explains the archaic use of the black swan as a metaphor. Europeans for centuries thought of black swans as being impossible because they had never seen one. Writers as far back as Aristotle used black swans as symbols for the improbable. Then a Dutch sea captain explored Australia at the end of the seventeenth century and what did his crew find? Black swans.[20]

For Taleb, the device works well. Just because we don't see a risk around us doesn't mean it doesn't exist. Since the swan serves as a foundational analogy for the entire book, Taleb takes the time to tell the tale.

Determining Fit

The explanatory power of the analogy derives from the truth it reveals.

Business authors love to use analogies in their titles and as foundations for their books: *What Color Is Your Parachute? Crossing the Chasm. Barbarians at the Gate.* They are not alone.

Jonathan Haidt's *The Happiness Hypothesis* likens the different mental systems we use to make decisions to an elephant and its rider. He writes:[21]

The mind is divided into parts that sometimes conflict. Like the rider on the back of an elephant, the conscious, reasoning part of the mind has only limited control of what the elephant does.

Haidt uses this metaphor throughout the book to frame his discussion of the irrationality of human behavior and potential approaches to happiness.

The image works well; although we never may have ridden an elephant, we can *imagine* what the experience might be like, and the potential mismatch between our strength and the elephant's. This inner picture helps us understand the limits of our rational, thinking minds in controlling our behavior and desires.

Foundational analogies are particularly tricky. In searching for a foundational analogy, we can overreach.

I wrestled with an analogy when writing *The Writer's Process: Getting Your Brain in Gear.* In describing the multiple steps involved in writing, the idea of baking bread came to mind. At first glance, the activities corresponded well. Both include several steps and rely on unseen processes to work while you'd doing other things. Bread bakers leave dough to rise, in the right conditions. Writers incubate their work, again in the right conditions, inspiring creative thought. Both writing and baking bread are a lot of work, interspersed with periods of rest.

By one set of measures, it was a great analogy: It involved sensory images such as aroma and the tactile work of kneading. The connotations were positive.

But when I tried to expand it to structure the book, I ran into problems of familiarity and fit. How many people bake bread? Also, the phases of writing didn't align perfectly with the steps of baking. Sure, research is like gathering ingredients, but at a certain point the analogy started falling apart.

No analogy is perfectly aligned with your subject, *especially* if the image is itself a complex process. I retained bread baking as a comparison, but downgraded it from a foundational analogy to a one-time explanatory one.

It doesn't really matter how much *you* love the analogy. Your reader will judge.

Methods for Writers: Choosing Analogies

In choosing an image or comparison, first determine what you're trying to achieve.

What type of analogy do you need?

Are you trying to illustrate a specific point or topic? If so, don't stress about a perfect fit. You only need a comparison strong enough to make the point, and perhaps jog the reader's memory if you refer back to it later.

Are you staking your entire argument and structure on the inferences drawn in the comparison? In this case, you'll have to think it through carefully, assessing the fit. Some analogies start out well, but get awkward or tiresome if pursued too diligently.

Search for the right analogy

Finding the right metaphor is an exercise in creativity. For inspiration, survey what others have done in your area.

Check out Metamania, an online database of analogies across diverse subjects. For example, I found an entry that compared using the Unix operating system to driving a stick shift car. The database is the brainchild of Metaphor Lab Amsterdam.[22]

Even as you get inspiration from others, remember that much of the power of an image comes from its novelty. Seek out unexpected associations and patterns, thinking broadly rather than deeply about your topic. In short, you've got to be creative.

If you're a numbers person rather than a creative type, don't panic. You're probably great at seeing patterns in numbers. Now find patterns in the world around you.

- Brainstorm a bunch of comparisons to your subject. Keep a list of possible topics—even ones that clearly won't work. They may spur other ideas that do fit.

- Let your mind wander on the topic when you're doing other things for a few days, and see if better examples percolate. (You'll be using the *incubation effect*, or the brain's tendency to keep background mental processes working on unfinished creative tasks.) For novel comparisons, contemplate unrelated fields.

- Be alert for fleeting thoughts and connections and write them down as they occur. By welcoming and encouraging these thoughts, you increase the chances that your brain will continue to chip in ideas when you're doing activities other than writing.

Don't neglect the library or your own bookshelves as a source of inspiration. Your creative contribution might lie in finding and repurposing an analogy in a new or compelling way.

Remember the elephant and rider metaphor that Jonathan Haidt used in his book? It worked so well that Chip and Dan Heath referred to it (giving full credit) in their book *Switch: How to Change Things When Change Is Hard.* They used the image of the elephant and rider to frame their principles for supporting change. Consider repurposing a great analogy from elsewhere, if you give credit to the source and it hasn't yet become a cliché.

Evaluate and test the analogy

As reader, nothing is more frustrating than encountering an analogy that doesn't make sense. Instead of being mildly puzzled, you are now doubly confused, and will either feel stupid or (more likely) curse the author.

Find a few people who represent your audience and test out your analogy. Ask for a reaction. Make sure that the comparison makes sense for people other than you. Don't cling obstinately to an analogy that doesn't work.

Also, remember that the images you choose may resonate with readers' memories and emotions in ways that you don't anticipate. Using words or images loaded with negative connotations can backfire.

Rules for testing analogies

When choosing an analogy, ask yourself the following questions:

1. Is the subject of the comparison familiar to the reader?

2. Is it possible the reader has an entirely *different* experience of the subject? Beware of negative emotional reactions.

3. Does the analogy really fit your topic, or are you stretching it to make it fit?

9

STORIES

Storytelling as an innate human activity
What's going on in the brain when we hear a story
How a single scene can imply a larger narrative
Illustrating abstract concepts through anecdote

I do not consider myself a storyteller. If a young child asks me for a story, I freeze up and stammer, or look around desperately for a book to read to them instead. In college, I practically ran and hid whenever anyone uttered the phrase "creative writing." (As an English major, this tendency led to awkward moments.) I preferred *reading* fiction to writing it.

So a few years ago, when storytelling became the hot new trend in marketing, I decided to research story techniques. And boy, oh boy, can it be daunting! You've got Joseph Campbell's *The Hero's Journey*, the three- or five-act story structure, and Freytag's pyramid. According to various sources there are only seven basic plots (or six, or nine). Your story needs inciting moments, rising action, a climax, falling action—ack! I felt my college creative writing phobia kicking in. My usual, deep-dive research approach to learning wasn't working.

Like a physicist trying to describe the act of walking, these theories of story systematize a natural part of the human condition. So I reframed the way I thought about telling stories, starting with the smallest moments, and practiced using brief anecdotes or scenes in my writing. I'm no master, but have faith in my ability to improve.

Although studying the craft of storytelling *will* make you better, the sheer magnitude of advice might prevent you from getting started in the first place. That would be a missed opportunity.

Stories can introduce concepts, engage curiosity, or guide readers to make important connections with their own lives. If you avoid anecdotes altogether, you'll miss out on a valuable writing tool. When it comes to helping people learn and remember, story is a powerful writing technique.

It's not as hard as you might fear.

The Science of Story

Toddlers don't learn to walk by listening to instructions: "Pick up the left foot—no, the *other* left. Now swing it forward and transfer your weight." Rather, they take small steps, experiment, and see what feels right. They fall a great deal, keep trying, and figure it out over time. We have evolved to walk on two feet.

Similarly, we have evolved to scan the horizon for cause and effect and to learn from the scenes we see unfolding around us. Our brains are constantly creating narratives, telling us stories about our lives.

Psychologist Michael Gazzinaga has identified a brain region that he calls the Interpreter that creates narratives to explain our behaviors. It resides in the left hemisphere of the brain.

Gazzinaga has done extensive research with "split-brain" subjects, or people for whom the connections between the left and right hemispheres of the brain had been severed (in a surgical attempt to treat epilepsy). These subjects embody the old phrase "The right hand doesn't know what the left is doing," but with brain hemispheres.

Gazzinaga designed experiments to induce the subjects to make simple choices or actions based on information available to only one of the two hemispheres of the brain. For example, he might flash a word that was visible only to one side of the subject's brain, then ask that person to point to a picture based on that word. If the left hemisphere saw the prompt, the subject had no problem explaining why they made their choice, as the Interpreter also resides in that neighborhood. If the right hemisphere saw the prompt and guided the choice of picture, however, then the Interpreter had no background information, since it resided in the opposite brain hemisphere. Yet the subjects always came up with a coherent story to justify their decision. The Interpreter gave it a shot. More telling, the subjects truly believed what they were saying. The person acted first, then came up with the post hoc reason for the action. According to Gazzinaga,[23]

This system is continually trying to keep the story coherent, even though these actions may be coming from processes outside our conscious awareness.

Some part of us is constantly constructing a narrative of our lives, creating reasons and plot lines that make sense of our experiences. Creating narratives comes naturally.

So does listening to other people's stories. In his lab at the Neuroscience Institute at Princeton University, neuroscientist Uri Hasson connected people to functional MRI scanners and tracked their brain activity as they listened to stories. He then compared the scans of multiple people listening to the same tale—and they lined up, not only in the auditory and language processing areas, but also in *other* parts of the brain engaged in listening, such as the frontal cortex.[24]

✴ Stories synchronize our brains.

What's more intriguing is that the patterns of the story*teller* line up with those of the listeners. If you were to listen raptly to me telling the tale of my latest vacation, our brains would activate in similar areas and timing. Hasson refers to this synchronization as *neural entrainment*. Our brains appear to be wired for creating and sharing stories. ✴

Story is a powerful vehicle for sharing your ideas and thoughts with others if you want to be understood. To get better at telling tales, practice. Here's the important point: You can start quite simply.

Reframing the Way You Think about Stories

A story doesn't have to be a tightly constructed, three-act set piece with a complex plot, protagonist and antagonist, rising and falling action, and so on. When you're writing nonfiction, you don't have to mesmerize people with suspense. You might simply frame a moment, a scene, or a transformation.

Stories put complex ideas into a human scale. Anecdotes often become shared mental groupings of meaning that we refer to again and again. A short, one- or two-sentence tale can bring your point to life.

Robert Sapolsky, a professor of biology, neurology, and neurosurgery at Stanford University, undertook an enormous topic in his book *Behave: The Biology of Humans at Our Best and Worst.* This monumental, 800-page tome explores and analyzes human decision-making, zooming out from the brain's neurons at the moment of the choice, back in time through genetics, cultural influences, and evolutionary biology. Sapolsky achieves his goals through a combination of winning structure, storytelling, humanity and humor, and excellent descriptive and explanatory techniques.

Deep within the book, Robert Sapolsky shares a short, two-sentence story, borrowed from his colleague Claude Steele at Stanford. This brief scene takes the topic of the role of the amygdala in reinforcing stereotypes and turns it into a human moment. Here's the passage in its entirety from *Behave:*[25]

> Steele recounts how an African American male grad student of his, knowing the stereotypes that

a young black man evokes on the genteel streets of Palo Alto, whistled Vivaldi when walking home at night, hoping to evoke instead "Hey, that's not Snoop Dogg. That's a dead white male composer [exhale]."

That fifty-word tale doesn't span three acts or have a complex plot line. Instead, it describes a moment in time, with a specific setting and a single individual. The retelling encapsulates both tension and resolution. It makes real the idea of unconscious bias. This is a masterful example of using an anecdote to support and illustrate a point, with no flamboyant storytelling, character-development, or plotting skills required.

The story is expanded on more fully in Steele's book about stereotyping, *Whistling Vivaldi: How Stereotypes Affect Us and What We Can Do*. The same short story can illustrate a single point or anchor an entire book.

Considered in this light, opportunities for storytelling can be found everywhere, for nearly any subject area. Every nonfiction topic has natural points on which to hang an anecdote. Your own experiences might serve as fodder.

Scientists create theories and then test them. Every test could be a story. Technologists find a problem and create a solution for it—another plot line. Whether you're writing about technology, science, medicine, policy, or finance, narratives frame the abstract topic on a relatable, human scale.

Stories fill several purposes in writing about complicated ideas:

- They aid understanding by providing concrete details for abstract concepts.

- They engage different parts of the reader's brain, making the writing more interesting.
- They help people remember explanations and facts.

A story's power lies, in part, in how it lands in the readers' minds.

Connecting with the Reader's Brain

When you read a novel, you create a picture in your mind, establishing a setting, filling in necessary details, and connecting with the emotional context of the situation. That's one reason screen adaptations of popular books can be disappointing. We are all the art directors for our own imaginations.

Stories engage multiple parts of your brain beyond abstract reasoning, including:

- Visual and sensory processing areas
- Emotional systems
- Memories

Journalist and author Daniel Coyle expresses it wonderfully (with a Las Vegas simile):[26]

> We tend to use the word *story* casually, as if stories and narratives were ephemeral decorations for some unchanging, underlying reality. The deeper neurological truth is that stories do not cloak reality but create it, triggering cascades of perception and motivation. The proof is in brain scans: When we hear a fact, a few isolated areas of our brain light up, translating words and meanings.

When we hear a story, however, our brains light up like Las Vegas, tracing the chains of cause, effect, and meaning. Stories are not just stories; they are the best invention ever created for delivering mental models that drive behavior.

As an example, let's return to that short tale of the graduate student whistling Vivaldi on the street at night.

First, it has sensory hooks, including a visual setting. Even if you haven't been to Palo Alto, you can summon a mental image of a suburban street at night. As for the protagonist, you work with the salient fact that he was a young African American male.

As you process the account, visual centers in your brain activate to fill in details. You might see a streetlight, under which a young man walks on a deserted sidewalk beneath a canopy of trees. The auditory factor is a bonus: the music of Vivaldi. You might summon the sound of someone whistling a Vivaldi piece, like a snippet from "The Four Seasons" or (in my case) the Vivaldi *Gloria*.

Emotions also play a strong part, since this is a story about *fear*. The graduate student worries about an uncomfortable confrontation, which itself would be fueled by a stereotype founded on fear. There's a happy ending, because reason overrides fear. This anecdote perfectly fits the message of the chapter, which is that the frontal cortex can, in the right situations, prevail over the fear-based amygdala. We interpret that lesson on a level beyond the purely analytical.

Illustrating the Abstract

We think, theorize, and learn in abstractions, grouping and manipulating levels of detail and categories of things or ideas. Instead of accepting abstract concepts at face value, readers may evaluate and test them. They may look for experiences that either confirm or deny your theory. Why not provide those concrete examples in stories?

The whistling student story in *Behave* appeared in the book after a discussion about amygdala activation in the presence of rap music. As an example of subliminal cuing, hearing a specific music genre (rap music) can trigger instant, fear-based responses in listeners or, perhaps, a sense of connection.

The tale shifted the discussion from abstract research (*hmm, interesting*) to an emotional, human experience. Story anchors the detail that supports the abstraction.

Aiding Memory

As any marketer or politician will tell you, people remember *stories*, not data. If you believe that we are, at an unconscious level, constantly making sense of the world around us by creating narratives, this should come as no surprise. We use stories to encapsulate the things we learn, making them easier to retrieve.

When learning something new, we often rely on mnemonic devices to create and strengthen memories. The ones I remember using from my childhood stick with me because they embed the stub of a story. For example:

- I learned to identify the treble clef notes EGBDF using the saying Every Good Boy Deserves Fudge.

- To remember the scientific taxonomy of kingdom, phylum, and so on, I was taught: King Philip Came Over From Germany Swimming.

These mnemonics work because in learning them, you can store the data along with a short scene that you later recall.

Much later in the book *Behave*, in a chapter about the brain's innate ideas of "Us" and "Them," Robert Sapolsky refers briefly to the initial tale of the whistling graduate student. The first account was powerful enough that hundreds of pages later (and possibly many days, depending on your reading speed), you can recall the tale, along with its underlying lessons about unconscious stereotyping. The right stories are memorable.

Learning through Story

In the third year of medical school, students leave the well-known environment of the classroom and start rotations, practicing medicine in multiple specialties with real patients. They undergo a critical transition from the classroom to the patient's bedside or examination room. Storytelling can help budding physicians make this transition.

At the University of California, San Francisco (UCSF), students return to the medical school's campus between rotations, and can choose to take a class on public writing during these periods.

Dr. Louise Aronson, a geriatrician, professor of medicine, and prize-winning writer, started the Public Medical Writing class at UCSF. Students start by doing critical readings. They discuss mechanics, such as story structure, and how to write about medical situations without violating patient privacy. Then, during class time, they write about their own experiences during rotations, read their work to others, and critique each other's stories.

What does this have to do with learning medicine, you might ask? As it turns out, quite a lot. I spoke with Dr. Dawn Gross, a hospice and palliative care physician who has taught the course. (She is also the host of a radio show called "Dying to Talk," centered on discussions about end of life.) She has witnessed the transformative power of storytelling for these physicians-in-making.

Gross observes that the medical students doing rotations are at the very bottom of a hierarchical medical practice, and that storytelling helps them transcend that beginner's role, turning experience into expertise. "The purpose of this class is to help the students start to recognize their expertise, to show that they are witnessing and experiencing stories, their own as well as those of patients and families. In writing, they become experts of those encounters."

Creating narratives is a path to learning. Says Gross, "Students come to this course to learn a skill—writing. They come away learning to discover what they have experienced in these intense encounters through writing, getting a perspective they could not understand in the moment."

The act of sharing those stories is similarly powerful. "Universally, the students tell us that not only has the course enhanced their appreciation of reading as well as writing, but they feel the companionship and camaraderie of the group. By reading aloud and getting feedback, they realize that they are not alone, and develop resilience for the journey to come."

Some students continue the course as fourth-year medical students, and polish and submit a contribution to a journal. So, along with educating physicians who heal, UCSF is training physicians who can communicate with the world about medical issues, expanding their impact. Says Gross, "If I'm talking to six people, that's the size of the impact I can have. If I can change the angle to be relevant to a larger audience, then I can expand my impact. That's what public medical writing is about."

Storytelling anchors great public medical writing.

When Story Goes Wrong

Standing in front of the museum display case, I dialed the number on my audio guide that matched the number in front of me. I hoped to learn something about the device in this museum of technology. Instead, two actors started reading a scene about two people in a marketplace a few hundred years ago. It took them a while to get to the point, so I moved on. Another exhibit caught my interest, and I tried again. Instead of explaining the display, the audio guide featured a recording of an actor reading a letter from the device's inventor to his sister. Again, and again, I sought out facts and was given a story instead.

In this particular museum, the only English-language resource available was a recorded audio guide. My French is only *comme ci, comme ça*, and I knew that trying to read all the signs in French would be tiring. (Refer to the description of cognitive load.)

But because they insisted on leading with stories rather than facts, the recordings frustrated me.

Even if had I *wanted* to hear all the tales, spending five minutes listening at each numbered entry, I would have perished of starvation before leaving the museum. Putting aside the audio guide, I muddled through reading the signs in French, then recovered from the cognitive load with lunch at a café.

Stories are great in the right context, but they aren't the *only* way to communicate information. If someone asks you a question, don't be one of those people who respond with "Let me tell you a story..." instead of answering them directly. You might get away with it once, but not twice. If it's a constant pattern, people will avoid you.

I will, anyway.

Story selection also matters. A tale that doesn't specifically reinforce your meaning can work against you. Extraneous detail might mislead the reader. Our narrative brains search for patterns and find them, whether they are valid or not.

If you've ever visited Bryce Canyon National Park in Utah, you no doubt remember the giant rock pillars (hoodoos) that define the landscape. Geologists can explain how they are formed over the eras, pointing out the ancient seabed and pattern of erosion. But I challenge you to gaze at them and not see other shapes: enormous terra cotta warriors, unworldly chess pieces, and turrets of fantastical fortresses.

Our brains automatically search for patterns, even when we know logically they don't exist. Sometimes, pattern-matching processes happen beyond conscious thought. That same pattern-matching instinct leads us to create narratives.

We hear of an incident and almost automatically apply cause-and-effect reasoning. If you took a statistics class in high school or college, then you understand that the larger the data set, the better the possibility at determining correlation. But as a not entirely rational human being, you'll also be swayed by a single, powerful story: the child who developed autism shortly after receiving a regular vaccination.

Individual, vivid events can skew our senses of proportion and probability. They feed a cognitive fallacy called the *availability bias*, or, as behavioral economist Daniel Kahneman phrases it, "what we see is all there is." The thing that we last paid attention to takes precedence. We can visualize it, so we deem it more likely to happen.

Anecdotes can overwhelm the data, so select the tales that most accurately represent the reality.

Unless you are writing about the exceptions (as Malcolm Gladwell does in his book *Outliers*), choose stories that prove the point most clearly. People will remember the stories and forget the norms.

Methods for Writers:
Improving Your Storytelling Skills

Stories and anecdotes are essential parts of the nonfiction writer's toolkit, particularly when you deal in abstract or complex topics. If you lack a fiction-writing background or don't consider yourself a storyteller, that's OK. Build your skills gradually, based on your comfort level, topic area, and natural writing voice.

Here are a few guidelines.

Start small

Don't attempt a three-act play or try to weave a single narrative throughout your longer work if you're not comfortable doing it. Stories usually have a progression, but they can also represent a moment in time, rich in emotional context, like the tale of the student whistling Vivaldi at night. Perhaps you can sketch a quick scene that the reader can fill in.

Mine your personal experience

We tell personal narratives all the time, most frequently to our family and friends. Look for past experiences that illustrate or exemplify a point, and try them out on someone. Writing about your own perspective and experience will feel less like fiction writing.

Find the naturally occurring stories

Social psychologists have a rich source of stories at hand, because their research often entails creating scenes for participants to act out, like ready-made plays. Technologists can find anecdotes in the human impact of their work. Policy makers can describe the situations they are attempting to address in human terms when writing about topics on a global scale.

Even hard data can be presented as a story, if you tell the tale behind the research.

Unearth the anecdotes and details to make your writing more memorable and the complex easier to understand.

Practice

As with almost anything in life, you'll improve with intentional practice.

If you're not secure with this writing method, first try crafting short anecdotes in a journal or other private place, without the stress of showing them to others. When that feels comfortable, try one out on a safe audience of friends or family. Then take them further afield. By retelling the account, verbally or in print, you will gain insight into what works and what doesn't, where people get lost, and what they might find interesting.

Use stories judiciously

Remember the dangers of story; if a reader is waiting for an important point, don't make them wade through a long digression. Find the level that suits your personal voice as well as audience needs.

Public speaking experts Poornima Vijayashanker and Karen Catlin offer advice that applies to writers as well.[27]

> Don't take too long to tell your story... Otherwise, you're taking your audience for a ride on

'the sinking ship of storytelling.' You take so long to tell a story that your passengers decide to fling themselves   overboard because they don't want to go down with a sinking ship.

Three rules for reticent storytellers

1. Start small; consider crafting a short scene rather than a long tale.

2. Mine your own experiences.

3. Shorter is safer.

10

EFFECTIVE REPETITION

What writers can learn from public speakers
Using the written form to your advantage
Tactics for repeating without boring your readers

I have a dream that one day this nation will rise up and live out the true meaning of its creed, "We hold these truths to be self-evident, that all men are created equal." I have a dream that one day on the red hills of Georgia, sons of former slaves and the sons of former slave-owners will be able to sit down together at the table of brotherhood. I have a dream that one day even the state of Mississippi, a state sweltering with the heat of injustice, sweltering with the heat of oppression, will be transformed into an oasis of freedom and justice. I have a dream that my four little children will one day live in a nation where they will not be judged by the color of their skin but by the content of their character.

Most Americans recognize the source of the quote above as a speech by the Reverend Martin Luther King Jr. They may not know when it took place exactly (August 28, 1963), nor its occasion (the March on Washington). But they surely remember the words "I have a dream."

That phrase appears four times in the excerpt above, and a few more times elsewhere. It has become the title by which we know the speech, the hook on which we hang our memories of its message.

That's the power of repetition used intentionally.

As a general practice, most of us try to *avoid* repeating ourselves. In social contexts, we don't want to be known as the person reciting the same story all the time, or harping on about our work. When writing, we don't want to bore the readers, nor do we want to appear condescending, as if we're talking down to them by reiterating the key points multiple times.

But think twice about that aversion. The artful use of reiteration can make all the difference in being understood.

Repetition and the Distracted Reader

Most popular music on the radio has a chorus that repeats, unchanged, between each verse. The listener knows the chorus, and can join in if they want.

In contrast, much classical music from the eighteenth and nineteenth centuries, before the days of radio and recordings, began with a theme, then presented a contrasting, secondary theme, then developed both themes and then recapitulated the primary theme before closing. The music fan of the time was accustomed to listening and remembering the key melody, detecting variations, and recognizing the reprise as a movement drew to a close.

Most modern rock music listeners don't pay that kind of attention. They may be driving, or chatting with friends. Popular music often plays in the background, so the melody must be clearer, more straightforward. Familiarity contributes to the enjoyment.

So it is with writing. Some books and articles demand close reading, others may appeal to a larger audience who have less time and focus. Readers of the same work vary in their approaches; some will focus on specific chapters, while others skim quickly or read with their minds wandering.

If you want people to *learn* from your writing, repeat yourself. Repetition plays a proven role in learning and memory. If you want the words to stick, reword and revisit your key concepts. How much you do this depends on the audience and your objectives, as well as your personal style. Are you writing for the careful reader or the casual reader? Are you writing the equivalent of popular music, or symphonies that require the listener's full attention and focus? The answers to these questions will help you determine how much you should reiterate.

To understand the power of repetition, writers can learn from a group that studies, practices, and masters it—public speakers.

Repetition and Speaking

If you've ever tried to take notes during a lecture or talk, you realize that the speaker's words are ephemeral. We don't always catch each word the first time it is uttered. We get distracted. Or, we may listen but not truly process them, so they never make it to our short-term memory.

Before interviewing him for this book, I had the opportunity to hear Daniel Pink speak about his book *When: The Scientific Secrets of Perfect Timing*. He anchored his talk around a certain chronobiological pattern that reappears in the book: peak, trough, recovery.

He repeated this phrase several times: after introducing and defining it, after sharing different research, after telling a story. He asked the audience to repeat it along with him. This repetition never felt dull or condescending—and I surely remembered the pattern once the talk was done.

Unlike speech, written words stay firmly on the page or screen. This may lead you to believe that it's not necessary to revisit key points.

I've said this before, but I'm repeating it because it's important: If you want people to internalize and remember critical ideas, they need to encounter them more than once. I asked Pink about his use of this technique in writing. He replied, "I'm a firm believer in repetition. That's challenging in a book, but I make a conscious effort to reiterate key ideas throughout the text. Why? Often an idea doesn't sink in until you've heard it a few times." Repetition gives the seed of an idea the chance to take root.

Remember also that readers are often distracted. They may skim over text without letting it sink in. Pink says, "As much as it pains writers, many people don't read books from page one to page done. It's not my highest concern, but I want my books to be accessible to people who skim or who just read particular chapters."

Repetition and Writing Style

Effective public speakers craft their speeches around repeated words or ideas, and never make it seem dull. Writers can do something similar.

Many of the authors I spoke to reiterated this theme. "One of the things that has surprised me is how often you have to say some things over and over again for them to sink in," says Michele Wucker, author of *The Gray Rhino*. "Your reader may be distracted, or focused on a different sentence or clause that resonates in a way you didn't expect; but other readers will get irritated if you are repetitive. So you need to find ways to repeat that don't sound like repeating."

How do we reiterate key points without becoming boring? First, rephrase when you reiterate—you don't have to use the same words.

Use other previously mentioned techniques, including story and analogy, to revisit key points. Present details that illustrate and repeat the theory. Revisit key points with intention, adding value and nuance.

Once you've done that, take advantage of the benefits of the written form.

What Writers Have that Speakers Don't

Public speakers can alter their pitch and volume to vary delivery. They can use repetition to build excitement and involve the audience. Writers don't have those tools, but we have something else.

We can build repetition into the *format* of our work.

Depending on what you're writing, the physical format of the end result gives you many opportunities to revisit key phrases and points.

Use titles and subtitles to highlight the key points in the sections that follow. For the reader, an apt subtitle appears instructive rather than repetitive, even if it reiterates the key theme. Within a blog post, article, or book, subheadings add structural cues for people who skim, while simultaneously reinforcing key points.

Quotes from third-party sources put the ideas in other people's words rather than your own, presenting another subtle way to revisit a concept.

Printed materials may include callouts and sidebars, which can drill down into topics or offer optional information, all while repeating the main ideas. Because these items reside outside of the linear flow of reading, they won't register as being repetitive.

To conclude (and repeat), reiteration fuels learning and memory. We live in an imperfect world, and not every reader will absorb your words the first time they encounter them. Repeat with intention and variation. Get creative and find ways to add value while reinforcing the key lessons.

Methods for Writers:
Repeat with Intention and Value

Heed the advice of great speaking coaches: Repeat the most important points so that they're sure to get through to the reader.

Find the key points

In *If I Understood You, Would I Have This Look on My Face?* Alan Alda shares his Rule of Three for speaking about complicated topics. It has (appropriately) three parts:

1. Make no more than three points when speaking.
2. Find three different ways to explain a difficult idea.
3. Repeat an important point three times.

Repeat with value

Don't simply revisit; get creative about making repetition a valuable part of the text. Depending on what you're writing, consider using different structural elements.

- An executive summary at the start of the piece summarizes the key points without seeming repetitive.

- Many readers appreciate quick summaries or lists of key points at the end of chapters.

- Many prescriptive nonfiction books (aka "how-to" books) conclude sections based in theory with advice for taking action. This adds a practical component to a nonfiction book without bogging down the expository text, while also reinforcing the key points.

PART THREE

HOW TO NOT BE BORING

11

TONE AND STYLE

Differences between voice, style, and tone
Why conversational writing isn't really conversational
The deadening effect of jargon
Four easy ways to alter the tone of your writing

Picture yourself talking about your subject to a group of people who represent your ideal audience. They hang on your every word. You've found just the right balance of story and data, but you are also charming and engaging. Maybe you're funny, or trustworthy, or authoritative, or a little of each. You are the best possible version of yourself.

This is the public speaker's dream—and it's hard to do.

Psychologists tell us that when we watch a person speaking, much of their communication comes not from the words, but from body language and tone of voice. Try tuning into a television soap opera in a language you don't understand. Chances are, you can get the gist of the relationships quickly. The best public speakers use their physi-physical presence to attract and sustain your interest.

As a writer, all you have are words to convey that best possible version of yourself. You might think that puts you at a disadvantage, but that's not entirely true. You have a powerful advantage when writing that you don't have in speech: *you don't have to deliver in real time.*

Writers convey personality and tone through the ideas we present, the words we use to encapsulate those ideas, and the sentences and paragraph structures in which we put those words. Simple stylistic and mechanical decisions influence the reader's feelings about the subject *and* the writer. Yes, the reader's impression of you *does* matter to the work. Nothing kills the reader's curiosity or interest as quickly as a lecturing, condescending tone.

Your objective is to find the best version of your written voice for this particular audience and situation. Tone and style take root while you write, but come to fruition during revision and editing.

Voice, Tone, and Style

The words *voice*, *tone*, and *style* are often used interchangeably in discussions about writing. Merriam-Webster online is my go-to dictionary for quick checks while writing. It offers the relevant definition of *tone* as: "style or manner of expression in tone or speaking." So, tone is style?

Hang on. Equating tone and style obscures an important distinction about who's in control. Writing *style* usually refers to the mechanics of the writer's action, while tone implies the subjective assessment of that writing.

Style belongs to the writer, and tone to the reader.

For the purposes of our discussion, let's agree on the following definitions:

Voice: Your unique way of thinking and expressing yourself. Your voice emerges in your speech patterns and in unedited writing.

Tone: The impression or feeling that the reader perceives from your writing. It doesn't matter if you *intend* to convey a helpful, explanatory tone. If the reader interprets the piece as condescending, that's the opinion that matters to that person.

Style: The accumulation of the writing techniques and methods by which you communicate tone. Most people switch almost automatically between multiple styles in our personal lives: academic style, informal email style, texting style, parental style, etc. But we can get hung up on style when writing something for the general public.

You probably have a default, go-to writing style, the way that you've always written for specific situations. You may not pay attention to it, but you've got one.

A few writers hide behind their voices, claiming, "This is how I write, my style, so love it or leave it." Your innate writing voice is not your destiny. You have the opportunity to change the natural writing voice in revision, through the mechanics of style.

What Tone Do You Want to Convey?

To answer questions of writing style, start with the tone you want to achieve. What attitude are you trying to convey about the subject? What's your relationship to the reader?

An "academic" writing style assumes the participation of willing and committed readers who bring existing knowledge of the subject area. Readers participate for the knowledge gained; any pleasure in the reading experience is a bonus. Of course, reality may differ. Students glance through readings to guess if the material will show up on a test. Professors may churn out articles desperately with the sole thought of publishing in academic journals. But, in the ideal world, the academic style assumes a committed reader and a trusted writer.

An academic style may not get you far in the outside world, however. As the geochemist and geobiologist Hope Jahren describes in *Lab Girl*:[28]

> I have become proficient at producing a rare species of prose capable of distilling ten years of work by five people into six published pages, written in a language that very few people can read and that no one ever speaks.

When writing outside of an academic context, you cannot assume the same relationship with the readers.

- Your readers may have no idea who you are, beyond a quick perusal of an online biography or book jacket.

- Readers may approach your writing with the thought of solving a pressing problem, satisfying an idle curiosity, or whiling away a few minutes in a dentist's waiting room. (Revisit Part One for ideas on assessing the reader's context.) What attitude do you want to project in this case? One of a helpful guide? An expert from on high? A fellow traveler through a fascinating topic? Identify the tone you want to communicate, and then let that decision guide stylistic decisions.

Let's Talk about Conversational Writing

Human beings have been talking to each other for much longer than we've been reading. Our default means of communication is conversation. For that reason, a so-called *conversational tone* is often effective for communicating complicated or abstract ideas in a direct, person-to-person way.

There's confusion, though, about conversation and writing. I've seen people publish rambling thoughts with the defense that they're attempting to strike a conversational tone. Aiming for a conversational tone doesn't give you permission to transcribe informal speech and publish it. When it comes to mechanics, writing is nothing like speaking.

N. J. Enfield is a professor of linguistics at the University of Sidney and author of *How We Talk: The Inner Workings of Conversation.* His research reveals the universal roles of timing, interaction, and nonverbal vocalization in human conversation. Precisely transcribed extracts of ordinary conversations, pulled from life, are rife with repetitions, instances of *uh* or *um*, interruptions, and back-and-forth clarifications. Enfield writes:[29]

> When two people talk, they each become an inter-locking piece in a single structure, driven by something that I will call the conversation machine.

Real conversation has much more going on than simply words passing back and forth. Please don't write exactly as you speak. Readers need more clarity than that.

In an in-person interaction, we rely on physical cues, intonation, pacing, and nonverbal articulations to communicate. A change in pacing signals the approaching end of a sentence, for example, while "um" indicates that there is more to come. You're probably less fluid and coherent when speaking than you believe. Whenever I see a word-for-word transcript of a podcast interview I've done, I'm horrified by my ungrammatical sentence construction and vocal mannerisms. Yikes.

Writing isn't a one-to-one conversation between two people in real time. It's a unidirectional, one-to-many broadcast of information between individuals who are not present with each other. Readers cannot hear or interpret your body language or vocal nuances, or let you know when they need quick clarification.

Written words reassemble themselves in the reader's mind. In that act of reading and parsing the text, the easiest path to comprehension is often a tone that *mimics* a personal exchange. The reader "hears" your voice as if you were there, speaking with them, but without the messiness of real conversation.

Conversational writing is better, more efficient, and clearer than ordinary speech, but puts the reader at ease as if you were in an informal discussion.

A conversational style isn't your only choice as a writer. You might aim for an objective, journalistic tone, or a more elevated, formal tone. In the book *Clear and Simple as the Truth*, Francis-Noël Thomas and Mark Turner extol the virtues of a *classic style* of prose. The distinguishing attributes of this style, according to the authors, are the attitude of mutual respect between reader and writer and a sense of curiosity toward the subject.

Start with your desired tone, then make stylistic choices.

Four Key Variables of Style

Your default writing style is not fixed; it is an accumulation of writing strategies that you employ, and have learned and practiced over years. You can modify your natural writing style during editing and revision.

Many discrete elements contribute to your style, including whether you use semicolons and abbreviations, footnotes or endnotes, and so on. *The Chicago Manual of Style*, which has been guiding writers on stylistic mechanics for more than one hundred years, tops out at 1,100 pages and covers thousands of tiny stylistic decisions. So many decisions!

If you seek to change the tone of your writing during revision, you will generate the largest impact by working with these four elements of your writing style:

- Paragraph length

- Sentence structure

- Point of view (first-, second-, or third-person)

- Vocabulary (word choices)

Academic writing often features lengthy paragraphs, long and complex sentence structures, formal (third-person) point of view, and field-specific vocabulary or elevated word choices. Journalistic writing uses shorter sentences and a general vocabulary while maintaining a third-person point of view. An informal, conversational style uses shorter paragraphs and sentences, the first- or second-person point of view, and commonly understood word choices (which does *not* imply the words are dull).

No matter how lively your sentence structures, jargon can hijack the tone you intend to convey.

What Jargon Does to Tone

In 2005, a couple of students in MIT's Computer Science and Artificial Intelligence Lab (CSAIL) pulled a prank uniquely suited to their talents.

Fed up with the multitude of academic conferences soliciting and publishing papers in the computer science field, the students created a program called SCIgen that automatically generated computer science papers, complete with graphs and citations, using buzzwords and jargon. Then they submitted one of their creations to a conference—and it was accepted.

Although the students revealed the hoax (and the conference rescinded the invitation), the program they created attracted attention. It still lives on.[30]

The story doesn't end there. Students continued generating robo-papers to expose conferences with less-than-rigorous acceptance standards. Less honorably, other individuals submitted generated papers to journals to pad their resumes with publications. In 2014, The Institute of Electronics and Electrical Engineers (IEEE) and the journal publisher Springer pulled more than 120 nonsensical, computer-generated papers from their subscription services—papers most likely generated by SCIgen or a similar program.[31]

The SCIgen saga is a cautionary tale about the power of jargon to bamboozle those who should know better. If conference organizers were unable to penetrate the lack of sense behind the words, think of your poor readers.

The presence of jargon serves as an instant pass to the front of the line, a sign of membership. If people don't completely understand what they're reading, they suspect they should. Their sense of belonging may be threatened.

When you use unfamiliar jargon, you're claiming membership of a group and, potentially, excluding the reader. This works against you if you aim to project a tone of warmth, accessibility, or understanding.

Search out the jargon and buzzwords in your writing and determine if reasonable substitutes would suffice. If the terms truly belong, offer definitions for your readers, so they can be part of the group of people that understands the language. Language can reinforce a sense of shared identity.

Methods for Writers:
Adjusting Your Tone

If you're accustomed to writing in an academic or industry style, consider manipulating paragraph length, sentence length, point of view, and vocabulary during revision to alter the perceived tone of your words.

Paragraph length

How many facts or insights do you pack into each paragraph? Do the readers have to work through large blocks of uninterrupted text on the page? If the subject matter itself is dense, try lightening up on the visual density.

What would happen if you put a single point in a paragraph?

Paragraph length affects the reader's rhythm. Short paragraphs offer the reader a chance to process what they've been reading. Breaking up long blocks of text may be the fastest way to lighten the tone of your writing.

Sentence length

Higher education traditionally trains people to master elaborate grammatical structures. Aptitude tests for college or graduate school asked you to decode complex sentences. In classes, you dazzled your professors with your verbal gymnastics and powers of parallel sentence construction. Multiple dependent clauses highlighted the balanced and nuanced nature of your thoughts.

But once you leave academia, put those skills aside. Briefer sentences communicate more effectively, particularly for people reading online.

Point of view

Simply saying "you and I" instead of "the author" and "consumers" or other abstractions will make your writing more personal, and hence warmer.

Word choice

Vocabulary contributes significantly to the reader's perception of tone.

Are you choosing words that make the reader feel like an outsider? Return to the discussion about abstractions, and for each piece of industry terminology you use, ask yourself if it is truly necessary.

- If so, define it the first time, and use it in a clear context.

- If not, replace it with a more familiar term or explanation.

12

IMAGES AND IMAGERY

The difference between metaphor and simile in the reader's brain
How metaphors can mislead
What's hiding in figures of speech

What if you could move around and touch things while trapped inside an MRI machine, instructed to remain still in that tightly confined space? You can, in a way, if you read.

In one Stanford University study, graduate students in literature read excerpts from Jane Austen's *Mansfield Park* while confined within an MRI machine.[32] The experiment revealed that regions of the brain involved with movement and touch activating during reading.[33] When we read about an image, we visualize it. When we read about an action, we imagine performing it, readying our own muscles to do the same thing.

Likewise, images and sensory metaphors connect on a level beyond the executive functioning and reasoning mind. They involve the reader more deeply by interacting with diverse regions of the brain.

Nonfiction writers can leverage the power of images to connect with their readers' minds. Imagery doesn't have to be visual; it might involve the senses of smell, touch, sound, or taste. In English major terms, I'm referring to *imagery, figurative language,* or *figures of speech.* Imagery tells subtle stories that either reinforce or, perhaps, undermine the larger meaning we are trying to convey.

Images often show up as metaphors or similes. In case you've blocked out this part of your education, let's clarify a few terms.

A **metaphor** claims two things are the same when, taken literally, they are not. Returning to the famous speech from Shakespeare's *As You Like It,* Jacques exclaims: "All the world's a stage, and all the men and women merely players." That's a metaphor.

A **simile** makes the comparison explicit, usually with the words *like* or *as.* Rephrased as a simile, Jacques might say, "All the world is like a stage, and all the men and women are like players..." What you gain in accuracy, you lose in poetry.

Metaphors and similes are both methods of proposing **analogies** that explore similarities between two things. Chapter 8 covered the use of analogies as explanatory models for your topic. This chapter discusses analogies on a smaller scale, including metaphors and similes in figures of speech, imagery, and figurative language.

The Three Superpowers of Imagery

When it comes to explaining complex or complicated topics, figurative language is one of the most powerful weapons you can wield. (See what I did there? I used a metaphor.)

An effective image works on multiple levels:

- Making the written work more interesting
- Forging a deeper connection with the reader
- Revealing satisfying insights

You can succeed at the first objective, coming up with an unusual or intriguing metaphor, without hitting it out of the park on the other two. That's all right. Any amount of appropriate imagery makes your writing more interesting. Let's dive into these different levels of impact.

Level One: Grabbing the Reader's Attention and Interest

The tech industry loves metaphors: white hats, clouds, folders, memory, and more. The venture capital industry likewise has its unicorns, pivots, and hockey sticks.

Relying as they do on unseen concepts, the technology and finance industries can seem dull to people not familiar with them. So writers in these fields come up with more compelling terms and images to earn attention. Thinking in abstractions gets boring and mentally fatiguing. A strong image kicks things up a notch.

Metaphors have the added benefit of the element of surprise. Unlike similes, metaphors appear to claim that two things are the same, when clearly they are not. There's no qualifying "like" or "similar to." Nope, metaphors come right out and make an irrational claim, leaving you to sort out the meaning.

When you encounter a metaphor while reading, you might stop for a moment and regroup. The part of your brain that has been parsing the language is momentarily confused: *Well, this is unexpected!* Remember, surprise is one of the sources of curiosity. Unexpected metaphors can hook the reader, at least for a moment.

To explore the power and pitfalls of metaphors, let's use the example of the *unicorn* in the world of tech start-ups. If you work in the technology industry, you have certainly already encountered the term. If so, try to place yourself back in time. Imagine that you are scanning a blog post about venture investments when you read about a *unicorn.* Since this is the first time you encounter the image in this context, you stop for a moment, perhaps less than a second.

A unicorn? Aren't we talking about privately held companies? What happened?

Your mind may have been wandering while reading about income statements, but now it sits up and takes notice. As an educated person, you immediately realize that you've encountered a metaphor, and you're curious how it will be resolved. That spark of curiosity inspires you to continue reading.

The power of metaphors and similes to grab attention derives in part from their *novelty.* When used frequently, metaphors and similes lose the element of surprise. They evolve into one of the following:

- A commonly accepted shorthand abstraction, often industry jargon

- A cliché that sounds tired and unimaginative
- A figure of speech, or an image that is so ingrained in the language that we hardly notice we're using it

The unicorn, when applied to a start-up business, now belongs to that first category, as shorthand to refer to privately held companies valued at more than $1 billion. When the term was first coined, start-ups with these astronomical valuations were rare. A tech investor today will know exactly what you're talking about if you mention unicorns. A random person on Main Street may not.

Here's the tricky part: Whether an image is surprising and novel or an accepted term depends entirely on the audience. Not you, not your colleagues—*your readers*.

One reader's cliché is another's fresh insight. You and your colleagues may use a phrase repeatedly, but to someone unfamiliar with your field, it may require an explanation.

Level Two: Deepening Your Connection with the Reader

Let's return for a moment to your first encounter, as a reader, with the unicorn metaphor.

Your brain quickly rummages around to make sense of it:

What do I know about unicorns? They have a single horn. They're white. They are not real. Even in fantasy stories, they are extremely rare.

As you take this short survey of existing knowledge, multiple mental systems pitch in.

- Your visual systems deliver the picture of a unicorn.

- Your memory may furnish snippets of a Harry Potter story.

- The associative mental processes in your brain, intrigued, start searching for connections that make sense.

In decoding the metaphor, you employ not only the brain areas responsible for language processing and rational, cognitive thought, but also sensory regions, and possibly emotional responses. You construct meaning on multiple levels.

This is great news for the writer, because now you're invested in the reading. The image has succeeded on the second level, deepening the connection with you. But, what insight does the metaphor offer?

Level Three: Satisfying Insight

You may formulate a flash hypothesis: Perhaps these start-up valuations are too good to be true. Is that what the author is trying to say? You read on to see if your theory holds. You are curious, and want an answer. Now it's up to the writer to deliver.

The unicorn image could support several interpretations. Perhaps it means that these are truly magical companies, discovered only in moonlight by virgin investors. Perhaps they are exceedingly rare, or their virtues are fictional.

When using analogies in your writing, how much do you have to explain?

If you use a simile (this company is *like* a unicorn), you owe it to the reader to explain it. You cannot simply move on to another topic. The simile is like a setup for a joke. The reader waits for the punch line, or in this case, the explanation.

Because a metaphor is presented as a fact (this company *is* a unicorn), you can theoretically leave it to the reader to infer the meaning. If you do so, point the reader in the right direction. Otherwise, their explanation may not match your own, and they may not understand the very thing you're trying to illustrate.

Don't wait too long before explaining an unfamiliar metaphor. Impatience can outstrip curiosity.

According to extensive research (more accurately, a quick look on Wikipedia), the start-up unicorn metaphor originated in 2013 with venture capitalist Aileen Lee, now of Cowboy Ventures. She used the term in an article in the online site TechCrunch to define private start-ups valued over $1 billion. At the time, these high-value start-ups were nearly as rare as unicorns.

Now, unicorns are trampling all over the tech industry. The data analytics company CBInsights maintains an up-to-date Unicorn Tracker that currently tallies more than *200* such companies.

If you work in a fast-moving industry, a metaphor may have a short shelf life—all the more reason to clarify the meaning.

The Perils and Pitfalls of Imagery

The careless application of metaphors and images can have unintended consequences.

Participants in a study at Stanford University were given printed descriptions of a fictional city called Addison and asked to offer suggestions for solving the city's crime problem. The descriptions differed primarily in the metaphors used. In some descriptions, crime was described as "a virus infecting the city," while in other reports, crime was "a beast preying on the city."

The choice of metaphor influenced the proposed solutions.

Those readers exposed to the virus image suggested addressing the root causes, or "curing" the crime problem. Those exposed to the beast metaphor proposed actions related to hunting, such as trapping the criminals and enacting harsher punishments.[34]

Why does this happen?

Language is a fairly recent development in human evolution; the use of metaphor and simile in written language is newer still. The earlier, emotional systems in our brains don't differentiate clearly between figurative language and reality.

The human brain is an enormously complex entity, with things happening on multiple levels. As you read, part of your attention may be tracking movement in the room around you, looking for potential threats.

For example, what happens if you read advice that you should "stick to your guns" in your retirement planning? Although that seems like a harmless figure of speech, your visual memories may summon an image of a gun. Simply visualizing a weapon can put you slightly on alert, since the visual cortex, on one level, "sees" a gun. This can spark negative or positive reactions, including emotions, sensory memories, and fear. Your amygdala, which invokes the fight-or-flight response, may activate an aggressive or fearful reaction. Now you're thinking about investments with an attitude, however minor, of fear or aggression. Either stance could yield unwise financial decisions.

The same thing is true for metaphorical verbs. When we picture an action, *mirror neurons* fire in our brains. That's why visualization exercises work for athletes, performers, and nearly everyone. Our minds practice the action we imagine.

Metaphorical verb uses like "killing it" or "rolling over" may invoke subtle physical responses in the audience. Images and analogies often bring unexpected physical and emotional baggage with them.

Metaphors Can Mislead

Remember Sabine Hossenfelder, the physicist who ran a consulting service for amateur physicists? This branch of science deals with forces and particles we cannot see without specialized equipment, if at all. In writing about physics, science journalists rely heavily on metaphors to help individuals understand what's happening. Yet Hossenfelder finds that people seize on those metaphors too literally. She asserts that the true language of physics is mathematical, not verbal. She writes:

A typical problem is that, in the absence of equations, [people] project literal meanings onto words such as 'grains' of space-time or particles 'popping' in and out of existence. Science writers should be more careful to point out when we are using metaphors.

Methods for Writers:
Choosing Effective Images

Metaphors and similes liven up your writing, but take care when selecting images.

Choose familiar images

A metaphor or simile connects with readers only if it is familiar to them already.

Let's say that you're a physicist, and you want to come up with an image for a rare type of company to replace the unicorn. You might write, "This company is the Higgs boson of start-ups."

That might work for readers grounded in physics, but others may have to turn to Google to make sense of it. Plus, few of us can visualize this particle. So, the Higgs boson fizzles when used as an explanatory image, unless you're writing for an audience of physicists.

As always, success depends on the reader.

Watch out for negative or emotionally charged images

As previously mentioned, imagery connects to areas of the brain beyond the rational and sensory-processing frontal cortex. It may summon memories with positive or negative emotional associations or prompt the fight-or-flight amygdala response. Something as innocuous as a clown might set off an unexpected reaction from readers with coulrophobia (the deep-seated fear of clowns).

Hidden pictures in idioms and figures of speech

When writing to produce a conversational tone, you may rely on idiomatic expressions, which often add images we don't notice to the words. While idiomatic language sounds natural and unscripted, it can lead you into trouble if the images are problematic.

Negative images: Words related to warfare and weaponry crop up in the strangest places, like a "battle" against illiteracy or "taking aim" at poverty. Ouch. Even common verbs like *trigger* can trigger a reaction. Once analogies or metaphors morph into figures of speech, we lose sight of the cultural or emotional context they bring along with them.

Cultural biases: After the September 11 attacks in 2001, President Bush spoke about mounting a crusade against terrorism. The word *crusade* most likely held a specific, emotional meaning for him. To people living in the countries of the Middle East, however, the word recalled the historical Crusades, retrieving memories of deadly clashes in the name of religion and a pattern of Western imperialism. Cultural context matters.

Translation troubles: If your audience includes a large number of people who are not reading in their native language, excessive use of idioms can add cognitive load. "Raining cats and dogs" in English might become "temps du canard" or duck weather in French. Reading either as a nonnative speaker might be confusing.

Don't become too attached

Clinging to a metaphor for the wrong reasons can inspire hilarity, as in this runner-up submission to the 2017

Bulwer-Lytton Fiction Contest, from Tony Buccella of Allegany, New York:

> Although in the rusty tackle box of his mind he yearned to be a #3 buck-tail spinner, Bob knew deep down he must accept his cruel fate as a bottom-bouncer rig, forever destined to scrape the muddy bottom of the river of life.

Please note that contest entrants *aim* to produce the worst prose possible, and nothing makes an easier target than a terrible metaphor. So, well done, Tony Buccella![35]

More rules for metaphors

- Use metaphors or similes when they support the work and advance your cause.

- Don't assume that an industry-specific metaphor is familiar to a wider audience; either make the meaning clear through usage or define it explicitly.

- Watch out for any unintended cultural connotations or emotional consequences of the images you choose.

- Think beyond the visual. Imagery that involves scent, touch, or movement can be particularly powerful.

13

CREDIBILITY, HUMANITY, AND HUMILITY

Why trying to sound intelligent backfires
The risks of asserting credibility
The pratfall effect
The power of humility

Think about the nonfiction writers you most enjoy, whose works you read regardless of the subject. They often go beyond simply explaining their topics to form a deeper bond with you, as a reader. They show up as real human beings, and narrow the distance between their own expert status and your understanding. They treat you, the reader, with respect, and themselves with humility.

Humility disarms the reader and paves the way for deeper connections.

Being human and vulnerable feels risky. You may want to establish credibility, asserting your right to write. Be careful how you claim authority, or you might hurt your own cause and make the writing less effective. Going on and on about your expertise and qualifications can appear pompous, self-absorbed, and—dare I say—boring. Build trust and credibility by writing with humanity and humility while demonstrating your knowledge.

That sounds counterintuitive, right? So, before we discuss humanity and humility, let's dive into credibility.

Credibility: What Doesn't Work

Depending on your topic and context, establishing credibility may be critical. Unfortunately, by insisting on your qualifications, you may broadcast a tone you don't intend.

Writers often use the following tactics, whether with intentionally or not, to demonstrate their worthiness to readers:

- Reviewing their credentials in the text (especially the opening)
- Retracing their steps
- Claiming an "insider" status

Those strategies can backfire.

People who lead into their subject by writing about their credentials often seem self-absorbed. Unless the author is a celebrity, the reader is there to learn about the topic. They can find the writer's qualifications in the "About the Author" section.

Then there are the writers who retrace their steps in excruciating detail. They have spent so much time gathering supporting data and research that they flood the text with that information, demonstrating the work they have done. A linear recitation of activities can bore the reader who is not yet hooked into the topic.

Finally, there are the writers who try to sound like serious experts by writing in the language and style of others in the field, like an insider. This can flop badly, actually diminishing the reader's respect.

Trying to *sound* smart and accomplished makes you seem less so.

As evidence, consider my favorite research study: a paper published by the psychologist Daniel Oppenheimer, then at Princeton University, with the wonderful title "Consequences of Erudite Vernacular Utilized Irrespective of Necessity: Problems with Using Long Words Needlessly."[36]

The researchers explored the impact of language complexity on the reader's assessment of the writer. In one set of experiments, subjects evaluated application statements from prospective graduate students for English Literature studies. Researchers altered some of the essays, swapping out simpler words for longer ones.

The applicants associated with the modified, complex essays were deemed less intelligent than those who used simpler words.

In a related experiment, the researchers found two different translations of the same passage from the French mathematician and philosopher René Descartes' *Medita-*

tions. Both translations were written in the 1990s, but they vary in their degree of linguistic complexity.

Since reading philosophy is the ultimate exercise in processing abstract ideas, this research is particularly appropriate for our purposes. Here's part of one passage (translated by Stanley Teyman):

> Now (after first noting what must be done or avoided in order to arrive at a knowledge of the truth) my principal task is to endeavor to emerge from the state of doubt into which I have these last days fallen, and to see whether nothing certain can be known regarding material things.

And the comparable section, in a translation by George Heffernan:

> ..now nothing seems to be more urgent (after I have noticed against what were to be cautioned and what were to be done in order to reach the truth) than that I might try to emerge from the doubts into which I have gone in the previous days and that I might see whether something certain concerning material things could be had.

A panel of experts deemed the second passage to be more complex than the first. I agree. It took me two passes through that last sentence to assemble it in my mind.

After reading one of the excerpts, study participants rated the intelligence of the passage's author. Those who read the first, easier-to-read translation thought the author was more intelligent than those who read the more complex one. This correlation held true even for people told that the original author was Descartes, one of the formative thinkers in Western philosophy. Descartes' reputation didn't matter. An awkward translation knocked a few IQ points off the famous philosopher and mathematician. As Oppenheimer and his team describe their findings, they uncovered "a negative relationship between complexity and judged intelligence."

As it turns out, the easier you make it for readers to understand your topic, the smarter they think you are. Conversely, the more you make them struggle, the less they think of *you* (not themselves). The "Keep It Simple, Stupid" maxim applies here, with a twist. If you don't keep it simple, readers might think you're stupid.

When Credibility Brings Risk

The challenges of establishing credibility are not evenly distributed. Just ask Katie Orenstein, founder and CEO of the OpEd Project. She's on a mission to increase the number of underrepresented voices sharing their expertise about significant, complex issues facing the world.

Orenstein has contributed to the opinion pages of the *New York Times*, the *Washington Post*, and other major publications. The OpEd Project grew from her attempt to answer a simple question: Why aren't there more opinion pieces from women in these influential publications?

The question was worth pursuing because, as Orenstein puts it, "the fundamental role of op-ed pages is to vet experts ideas; opinion pages are a huge predictor of future policy. These are the essential source code for history." When *any* group's voices are absent from these forums, that group remains in the margins of history. The OpEd Project's tagline is "The story we tell becomes the world we live in."

Orenstein set out to test a pragmatic solution to this problem. At its inception, the OpEd Project taught people how to pitch opinion pieces for placement. It worked, to a point. Says Orenstein, "By increasing the pitching ratio, we've been able to have a tremendous impact on who gets published. But the problem didn't turn out to be writing or pitching. The real problem is deeper: we live in a world in which some people pitch with much greater frequency and success than others."

Credibility turned out to be the sticking point. According to Orenstein, "For people in underrepresented groups—such as women and minorities—asserting credibility is risky. For women, for example, competence and likability are negatively correlated. The risk is high and the reward is low, and people know it in their gut."

The OpEd Project has made it its mission to encourage the participation of a full range of human voices in public discourse. In its workshops, participants explore strategies for navigating the risks and challenges around establishing credibility. Says Orenstein, "It's not a safe, easy world. To do the things that matter, we have to step into the hard things that may happen. That doesn't mean we step in naively, or without strategy or intention."

Learn more about its seminars for individuals and organizations at TheOpEdProject.org.

The word *credible* means believable. To be believed, you must first be understood. The path to credibility lies in connecting with your readers authentically and earning their trust, or at least their attention and openness. To do that, consider appealing to common humanity.

Humanity

Human beings are social animals. We enjoy connecting with and hearing about other people. When you're writing about complicated or abstract topics, bring a person into view, even if that person is yourself.

You've probably heard the story of the discovery of penicillin, but I'll repeat it anyway. A professor of bacteriology at St. Mary's Hospital in London named Alexander Fleming took a holiday to Scotland in 1928. When he returned to his lab after vacation, he discovered mold growing on his petri dishes, which had killed the bacteria he'd been nurturing. Instead of tossing the thing away in disgust, he paid attention to the mold itself—and thus begins one of the wonders of modern medicine.

The story resonates with anyone who has ever come home from vacation to discover an emerging life form on the counter or in the fridge. It transforms Fleming from an unknown scientific pioneer of the past into a person with housekeeping standards we can relate to. Plus, the account brings microscopic entities into a human scale, holding lessons about the unseen world around us.

Science is often taught through the stories of the people making the discoveries, connecting abstract topics to real people. Nearly every topic has a human angle.

We listen to and believe people we know, like, or respect. Appearing as a real person in your writing helps you communicate about your topic. As the social psychologist and author Jonathan Haidt writes:

> Friends can do for us what we cannot do for ourselves: they can challenge us, giving us reasons and arguments that sometimes trigger new intuitions, thereby making it possible for us to change our minds.[37]

You can be present in the work via the words you choose and the stories you tell. If you are excited or enthusiastic about your subject, let it show in the writing. If you want to rant, *and* if you have earned the reader's permission and trust by delivering solid information to this point, you can let people know how you really feel.

You can easily take this too far. Readers will have varying degrees of tolerance for personal information. They may bring different expectations depending on the content. A memoirist has much more leeway for sharing personal stories than a reporter. Imposing yourself too much into your writing can make you seem self-absorbed, conceited, or condescending. So if you want to be human in your writing, add a dash of humility as well.

Humility

Writing with humility doesn't mean downplaying your credentials or weakening your credibility. Humility in writing is *not* false modesty, humble bragging, or compromising your authority on the subject. By humility, I mean two things:

- Admitting to human foibles (without bringing your subject expertise into question)
- Respecting the reader

Humility, done right, *enhances* credibility. Showing vulnerability can make you more likable, which will increase your effectiveness.

Adam Grant uses the term *powerless communication* to refer to a strategy of writing or speaking with humility and vulnerability. In his book *Give and Take: A Revolutionary Approach to Success*, he tells a story of teaching motivation strategy to senior military leaders—at the tender age of 22. His first attempt fell flat, so on the next try, he opened by saying:

> I know what some of you are thinking right now: "What can I possibly learn from a professor who's twelve years old?"

He poked fun at his own age, but not his expertise. As he tells the story, this self-deprecating humor did the trick: The senior leaders in the room were willing to hear what he had to say about motivation, and gave him high marks on the speech.[38]

The psychological term for this is *the pratfall effect*.

In the mid-1960s, social psychologist Elliot Aronson asked research subjects (all male college students) to listen to tape recordings of high school students auditioning to appear on a quiz show.[39] Of course, the tapes were the scripted products of the researchers, not recordings of actual quiz show candidates.

On each tape, the prospective contestants first described their academic qualifications (grades and activities), then answered trivia questions. Half of the contestants described themselves as average students and performed accordingly in their answers, getting almost as many questions wrong as right. Others claimed high grade point averages and superior accomplishments. These high achievers aced the trivia questions, and were thus prime candidates for a quiz show.

Some of the scripts included a line or two about spilling coffee on themselves—a kind of audible "pratfall" narrated by the contestant. "Oh no, I've spilled coffee on myself!" Remember, these were audio recordings, so the researchers didn't need incredible acting skills.

Study participants were asked to rate how likable the contestants were. The listeners (the actual research subjects) didn't always warm to the accomplished, high-performing contestants. They preferred the smart students who had made the unrelated gaffe, spilling coffee, to the other accomplished candidates.

The ability to hold a coffee cup steady has nothing to do with intelligence or trivia knowledge, so the spill didn't make the smart, accomplished candidates seem less smart and accomplished. It did, however, make them more human. The research subjects wanted to watch those candidates compete on the game show.

By making you more likable, displaying vulnerability can helps you earn attention and trust.

Respect is the other key ingredient in humility. When you respect the reader's intelligence and motives, you won't stray into lecturing or condescension. If you are considerate of the reader's time and attention, you'll avoid sounding pedantic.

When you think of the reader as your equal—perhaps not in subject matter expertise, but in other ways—you escape the curse of condescension.

**Methods for Writers:
Humanity and Humility**

Treat humanity and humility like spices in cooking: a little goes a long way. Experiment with finding the right balance for your personal voice, your readers' expectations, and the specific piece you're writing.

Credibility

You may need to establish your credentials to write about your subject. Beware of methods that establish a tone you do not intend. These include:

- Spending time on your own credentials and accomplishments instead of the main subject

- Adopting a "serious" tone in the mistaken belief that to be taken seriously, you need to sound serious

- Taking readers through the entire process of thought and research that led to your current view

- Relying on terminology and jargon to signal insider status

Earn authority and believability through other means.

Put your credentials in your author biography, outside of the main flow of the work. Winnow the biographical data to include things relevant to your expertise on this topic. Writing separate biographies is a small price to pay for not annoying your readers.

If possible, let *other* people talk about your qualifications.

Do a great job of explaining topics so the reader feels smart and informed. This will reflect well on your overall credibility.

Humanity

Offer your readers ways to connect with you personally, and they will be more receptive to what you have to say.

You might include relevant personal stories. As we've seen with the pratfall effect, a small dose of vulnerability can build the reader's trust. If you show up as a fallible and curious human being in your writing, readers are more likely to trust you.

You will have to judge whether it is appropriate to share a personal story, and whether you are comfortable doing so. Too much personal information can distract from the subject at hand. If you feel reluctant, start small with a short aside, parenthetical comment, or a personal note in the footnotes.

Humility

Humility is about narrowing the distance between yourself and the reader, finding common connections, and admitting imperfections. If you want to be understood, focus on being effective, rather than right. Respect your reader and your topic rather than insisting on respect.

Yes, there's risk involved in being human and humble. If executed well, these methods pay off. Consider self-deprecating humor, which is covered in the next chapter.

Rules to remember

Humanity and humility in your writing can reinforce, not erode, your credibility and effectiveness. The methods in this chapter support and enhance each other. Balance is the key. Keep these rules in mind.

1. Credibility is granted by the reader, not asserted by the writer. Earn it rather than insisting in it.

2. To connect more deeply with individual readers, give them a glimpse of yourself as a real person.

3. A small amount of vulnerability can help you earn the reader's attention or trust.

14

HUMOR

Theories of humor
What can you learn from John Oliver?
How humor enlists the reasoning mind
The humanizing effect of comedy

On his HBO show *Last Week Tonight with John Oliver*, comedian John Oliver regularly tackles complicated financial, scientific, and legal issues such as:

- Forensic science and its limitations
- Medical debt and predatory lending practices
- Net neutrality
- Argentina's debt crisis

These are obscure and potentially depressing topics, even for political comedians. Most episodes include a healthy dose of exposition and explanation to bring the average American viewer up to date on the subject.

Oliver's entertaining treatments often inspire action beyond the show. Viewers have overwhelmed government websites with submissions or incited lawmakers to introduce legislation to fix problems. A U.S. federal appellate court judge cited an episode of *Last Week Tonight* in a decision about taxes and U.S. territories. These stories contribute to what the press calls the "John Oliver Effect" and demonstrate the power of humor when dealing with complex issues.

Oliver has many assets that you and I do not, including a show produced by HBO, a talented team of writers, an established audience, a background in comedy, and *that accent*. To an American audience, Oliver's particular variety of British accent confers instant credibility.

Viewers tune in to be entertained by the jokes, and perhaps to inhabit a sense of righteous indignation over the wrongs of the world, or to satisfy curiosity about topics we knew nothing about.

So, what's going on here? How can these esoteric and downright depressing topics be funny?

The Science of Humor

Humor, as a field of research, belongs to many disciplines. If you want to explore the science behind it further, you might start with *The International Journal of Humor Research*, which publishes studies from many disciplines including anthropology, biology, education, gender studies, linguistics, philosophy, political science, psychology, and sociology.

Let's start with the two-part theory of humor published in that journal in 1998, titled "A Theory of Humor."[40] The author, Thomas Veatch, posits that to be funny, a joke must 1) violate a subjective expectation, and 2) still represent a normal situation. Apparently, Veatch's favorite joke[41] was

Why did the monkey fall out of the tree?

Because it was dead.

So yes, humor is subjective. That wouldn't rank as my favorite joke. But it illustrates the theory. The question sets up an expectation. The answer is unexpected but still works. It resets our expectations to a new normal. That's the origin of every knock-knock joke and bad pun ever told.

The listener's smile or chuckle (if there is one) arises from the brain's fast action to resolve the unexpected contradiction. A joke is funny only if we can make sense of it, and quickly. The answer doesn't give us joy by itself—our *understanding* of it does.

Journalist and author Jamie Holmes describes it beautifully in his book *Nonsense: The Power of Not Knowing.*[42]

> For puns and jokes, laughter is a testament to the voracious power of our sense-making minds, as all three of the processes involved—expectation, surprise, and the discovery of a rule that resolves the puzzle—happen almost instantaneously. ... Chuckling also springs from our exploration of hidden meaning and our delighting in clever, unexpected connections that we normally disregard.

188 WRITING TO BE UNDERSTOOD

Another, in-depth exploration of humor can be found in *The Humor Code* by behavioral scientist Peter McGraw and journalist Joel Warner. The book combines the research and road trip genres while delving into the essence of comedy. McGraw refines Veatch's thesis with his own *benign violation* theory: We find things funny when they violate our expectations *and* are not inherently threatening or damaging. In a way, laughter signals socially that everything is fine.

How can that help us when writing nonfiction about unfunny topics?

Using Humor to Explain

Humor helps us make sense of unexpected situations. It is therefore a natural ally for the author trying to explain the unfamiliar, since it enlists the sense-making part of our brains. Like analogies, humor shifts the reader's perspective, often revealing an unexpected truth about the topic.

In his book *Astrophysics for People in a Hurry*, Neil deGrasse Tyson attempts to describe the strange relationship between the laws of gravity and quantum physics in this way: [43]

> In the beginning, during the Planck era, ... we suspect there must have been a kind of shotgun wedding between the two.

The shotgun wedding is an unexpected analogy that is both amusing (a trademark of Tyson's personal style) and illustrative. We don't quite know how these two forces ended up hitched, but that union begat the universe as we know it. Humor can make the unknown (like quantum physics) accessible; an unexpected metaphor simultaneously lightens the tone and enlightens the reader.

Making Emotional Connections

The power of humor goes beyond explanation to emotion. Remember the "benign violation" theory of humor? In this view, the punch line of the joke signals that everything is OK.

Laughter alleviates the tension inherent in serious topics or stress-filled settings—even settings associated with gloom and illness. Canadian researchers interviewed patients, families, and staff in intensive care and palliative care units to survey the role of humor in medical care. They found that levity has many positive side effects, including personalizing healthcare delivery and reducing patient embarrassment. The researchers concluded that "combined with scientific skill and compassion, humor offers a humanizing dimension in healthcare that is too valuable to be overlooked."[44]

Humor *humanizes* by exposing the common ways our brains work, creating connections between writer and reader or speaker and listener.

Self-deprecating humor can have a similar effect. A small dose makes you seem more human. It narrows the perceived distance between yourself and the reader, as the research about the pratfall effect in the previous chapter suggests.

If you poke fun at yourself, others are less likely to take offense. Just don't do so in a way that undermines your credibility. Focus on areas unrelated to your expertise (say, your height), or tell a story from earlier in your life, when you were less wise than you are today.

Methods for Writers:
Adding Humor to Your Personal Style

Using humor effectively is one of the toughest (and riskiest) writing strategies in this book, which is why it appears near the end of the book. Unless your goal is to become a stand-up comic or write a long-running comedy series, it doesn't take much to have an impact on your writing.

Think fun, not funny

When it comes to adding humor to your writing, don't try too hard. To quote my friend Kathy Klotz-Guest, who is a genuinely funny person in addition to being an author, speaker, stand-up and improv comedian, focus on *having fun* rather than being funny. "People fundamentally misunderstand what humor can be. Everyone thinks *I have to be funny*. On the improv stage, if you're trying hard to be funny, you will fall flat. Being funny isn't the most important thing—having a sense of fun is. Fun makes a big difference in writing. You can't get to funny without fun."

Start with short and sweet

As with storytelling, you can start small and gradually expand your expertise and comfort level. Some serious authors bury amusing comments in their footnotes, for those dedicated readers who venture there.

Humor in your writing might show up as a simple aside, a play on words, or an entertaining metaphor. In *Dollars and Sense*, by Dan Ariely and Jeff Kreisler, the humor is sprinkled throughout, often in asides like the following:[45]

> In a recent branding study, people with too much time on their hands—also known as 'volunteers'—were asked to try out products.

Learn from John Oliver

I've picked up a few strategies by analyzing *Last Week Tonight with John Oliver* and extrapolating lessons for writers.

Timing is critical. Each *Last Week Tonight* segment is about twenty minutes long, but it's never one uninterrupted diatribe. Camera angles change and Oliver paces his verbal delivery. He keeps the tone light, while breaking the exposition into smaller segments to sustain the attention of the television audience.

Vary perspectives. Guest stars often appear in video clips, creating mini-anecdotes to illustrate the absurdity of a situation. In writing, you can create "guest star" appearances through quotes or stories.

Use an upbeat ending. Oliver frequently ends segments with that most potent ingredient of all—*hope.* He closes with a suggestion for making the world better. In the segment on medical debt, he concluded by announcing that he had started a nonprofit fund that had purchased and forgiven $15 million in medical debt.

When humor combines with hope, great things can happen.

Humor hints

- Aim for a smile rather than a guffaw.

- Deploy humor in service of the content, not the other way around.

- Focus on the positive; remember the role of humor for signaling that everything is OK.

Writing Advice
from a Comedian

Name: Jeff Kreisler
Experience: Lawyer, speaker, author, comedian
Special skills: Infusing topics like finance and human behavior with humor

---

I first encountered Jeff Kreisler's sense of humor when reading *Dollars and Sense*, the book he co-authored with the cognitive scientist Dan Ariely. I reached out to Jeff to ask him for his advice on using comedy when explaining topics like behavioral economics and finance.

The role of humor in nonfiction writing

The first question was, of course, why write a book that combines financial decision-making advice with comedy? What does humor bring to the topic?

Says Kreisler, "Humor engages and disarms people, and that's particularly valuable when you're writing about complex, confusing, or threatening topics. The end of a laugh is followed by the start of a listen."

Understand the audience

The reader is the ultimate judge of whether or not something is funny or amusing. When he speaks to a group or writes speeches for others, Kreisler always asks the event organizers in advance for detailed information about the audience.

For writers, visualize the people you're trying to reach in a personal way. Kreisler suggests, "Imagine yourself sitting and talking with friends or colleagues explaining your topic. The best sources of humor are the comments that would make them chuckle or smile. If you think something is funny but would alienate or anger someone in that setting, don't use it."

Sources of humor

When using humor to illustrate your topic, find inspiration in unrelated but familiar areas. "The best sources of humor often appear when you step back from the topic and try to relate it to another sphere of life. Analogies are often entry points into humor."

Mitigate risks

Because Kreisler writes about risk and decision-making, it seemed fair to ask him about the risks of using humor in writing.

Kreisler, as a rule, leaves the risk-taking to the stand-up comics, not the professional writers and speakers. "When writing in a professional setting, if you think there's a chance something isn't appropriate, don't do it. You don't have to be funny. Humor that derives from meanness, aggression, or anger rarely has a place in this kind of writing."

Balance humor and exposition/explanation

Kreisler advises against trying too hard. "When you're writing to explain, you don't have a mandate to be funny every ten seconds, like a stand-up comic. If there's a joke opportunity but it's not appropriate, don't use it."

How do you determine how much is right? "I look at the density of humor on the page and decide how much to leave in. It's more important to be credible and useful than funny."

Getting the balance right isn't easy. "Be prepared to edit and rewrite. Have other people give you their honest feedback. Don't try to force the humor. Sometimes you have to 'kill your darlings' if a joke won't work."

Get help

If necessary, hire a professional to punch up your prose. Says Kreisler, "Comedians are often smart people who lacked the focus to get a specific advanced degree, or (cough, cough) to use it. [Kreisler has a law degree gathering dust.] Consider enlisting help."

15

FINDING YOUR PERSONAL STYLE

Sorry, there are no formulas
Improving on your default writing style

When I started talking with people about this book, many eagerly told me about *their* favorite nonfiction books and authors. My reading list grew by leaps and bounds and I discovered many wonderful works. Despite the enthusiastic recommendations, I didn't love them all. Our tastes are different.

You face a choice: write only for the subset of readers predisposed to love your writing, or take steps to broaden the impact of your message. This book gives you the keys to do the latter, while connecting more deeply with the readers you already have.

Even if you master every method here, you won't reach everyone. The art of nonfiction lies in finding a balance that suits your audience and becomes your personal style.

There Is No Formula

Pick up a book by one of your favorite nonfiction authors. Instead of getting caught up in the words, keep your distance and identify the techniques the author uses. You'll find:

- Stories
- Explanatory analogies
- Humor
- Personal anecdotes revealing vulnerability or humility
- Figurative language

Search out the various techniques described in this book. Once you look for them, you'll start seeing them everywhere.

Now find a different book by another author you admire. You will detect the same writing methods used in different combinations.

Occasionally, I sense an author adhering to a specific formula or set of rules that remains constant throughout a book, such as:

- Start every chapter with a story.
- Cut back and forth between the anchoring story and the background explanation three times in each chapter.

- End each chapter with a teaser about three stories you will share in the next chapter.

These formulas are like training wheels. They take you only so far, and at a certain point, they'll get in your way. Plus, people might notice—especially the ones who, like me, study this stuff.

I cannot give you a story-to-data ratio, nor tell you how many metaphors to use per thousand words. There is no single formula. You'll have to find your own balance.

Student teachers are taught to accommodate various learning styles: visual, auditory, kinesthetic, verbal, etc. As an author, you may think that you are confined to one way of reaching people: through reading. Even among devoted readers, some people respond to stories, others to data, and others to an apt analogy that resonates with them. In seeking to be understood, we face the wide variations of the human condition.

The most adept writers combine techniques to reach more people. If your audience is broad, you may need to use multiple methods in this book to catch people's attention, communicate your message, and retain their interest.

By exploring and experimenting with the ideas in this book, you can balance your readers' needs with your comfort level and natural writing voice. Over time, you will refine a personal writing style that works for your audience, your topic, and your sense of self.

Your Personal Style

How would you describe your writing style today? Do you want to alter it to reach more people?

Too often, we write the way we've always written without regard for how it appears to the reader. As Francis-Noël Thomas and Mark Turner write in *Clear and Simple as the Truth*:[46]

> Style is like the typeface in which a text is printed. We may overlook it, and frequently do, but it is always there.

In this book, you've encountered ways to explain abstract topics, such as using analogies, anecdotes, and repetition. You've surveyed methods for sustaining the reader's interest, including appealing to innate curiosity, using figurative language, and infusing your writing with humor and humility.

With self-reflection and a willingness to experiment, you can adjust your style to reach a broader audience or connect more deeply with your readers.

The way that you mix and blend these tools becomes part of *your* personal nonfiction style. You will vary and adjust that style based on the reader's needs, but at the core, you're the one making the decisions. If a writing method feels awkward or not "like you," then it's not your style. If you aren't comfortable using personal anecdotes, don't tell stories from your experiences. If you feel cheesy repeating your key message, then don't do it.

Experiment, explore, and see how your writing lands with the readers. With practice, you may discover new depths in your writing, and your style may evolve.

Where We Go From Here

After a career writing about complicated technologies for a business audience, I *thought* I understood this topic. Then I started studying the work of other nonfiction writers more closely and exploring the cognitive science behind understanding. The more you learn, the less you realize you know.

Writing this book has changed the way I read nonfiction, since I cannot help mentally labeling the writing methods as they whiz past. (Humor! Personal anecdote! Clever analogy!) I now see the forest *and* the trees, switching perspective with disconcerting regularity.

This change in reading habits is a small price to pay for a window into the skills and habits of terrific writers. I've always relied a great deal on my gut instincts when writing. Working on this book has made me realize how difficult it is to apply these tactics in a studied way without feeling forced or formulaic.

The best authors balance intentional craft with compassion for the reader and insight into what works for them. By practicing and deploying the tactics in this book, I am refining my own writing style. I hope you experience the same thing.

What's Next? The Call to Action

My marketing background compels me to close with a call to action (CTA in marketing jargon). Marketing writing often attempts to manipulate human behavior to a specific end, like "download the white paper," or "click the Buy button," or "leave a book review."

(Seriously, I wouldn't mind if you left a book review.)

Here's my call to action for you: Select a few methods from this book and adopt them in your writing. You're probably already doing most of them, but see what happens when you use these techniques with intention. Experiment.

If you have read this far, writing must be important to you. Whether you're a scientist, historian, policy wonk, technology geek, researcher, philosopher, or a deep thinker who wants to share your ideas, it's up to you to figure out what to do with the advice you've encountered in these pages.

I trust that you won't abuse these tactics to manipulate people. The world desperately needs reasoned discussion about complex issues. So, do what you can to foster and contribute to productive, respectful discourse and discussions. Go forth and write.

ACKNOWLEDGMENTS

Countless nonfiction writers and authors have inspired me over the years, too numerous to mention. But a few deserve a special call-out for their generous contributions of time and expertise to this work. My deepest thanks go to Daniel Pink, Nir Eyal, Jeff Kreisler, Dave Gray, Michele Wucker, Ellen Cassidy, and Steven Sloman for spending time to clarify my thinking and for contributing directly to the insights in these pages.

This book is also the product of numerous lively conversations with writers across diverse industries. Not all of those interviews appear in the book, but each strengthened my understanding of the topic and made the work better.

I am fortunate to be part of an incredible group of smart and supportive women authors, to whom this book owes a great deal. Sarah Granger, Michele Tillis Lederman, and Cindy McGovern have each contributed their insights. Linda Popky remains one of my go-to sources for advice, and this book is no exception to that rule. Michele Wucker generously shared her time and perspective, and then connected me with others who expanded my understanding of journalism, including Katie Orenstein of the OpEd project and Susy Schultz of Public Narrative. Countless others in this group offered essential advice and encouragement; thanks to all my fellow authoresses.

Laura Lindenfeld of the Alan Alda Center for Science Communication at Stony Brook University was incredibly helpful, sharing insights and research into the role of improvisation in scientific and medical communication. To Dawn Gross I owe the story of public medical writing and its impact on medical students—a topic I would not have understood without her unique perspective.

The coffee shops of the Bay Area were abuzz with conversations about writing in preparation for this book. As I chatted with Kathy Klotz-Guest, unsuspecting customers were regaled with our conversations about improvisation and humor in writing. In separate caffeinated conversations, Poornima Vijayashanker and Karen Catlin shared their expertise in speaking and writing in the technology industry. And if you want an entertaining coffee conversation, meet up with Ellen Cassidy to talk about logical reasoning and writing. You won't be disappointed.

My publishing team has significantly improved the quality of the work. Laura Duffy's excellent cover design alone raises the standard for quality. I rely heavily on Laurie Gibson's editing (and moral support) and Mark Rhynsburger's proofreading—any mistakes that slip through are entirely on me. For her continued publishing advice and wisdom, I am indebted to Holly Brady. Chris Syme's level-headed book marketing advice is always valued. Roger C. Parker, Ginger Weeden, and Renee Rubin Ross have likewise offered suggestions that improved the work.

The many people who participate on my Writing Practices email list serve as a constant source of inspiration. They share encouraging words and keep me tightly focused on delivering value to the readers I want to reach. They fuel my writing, and I never take that for granted.

I'm also particularly lucky to come from a nonfiction-loving family of readers who readily share their favorite authors and books. My mother keeps us well supplied with the latest titles, and my siblings swap recommendations for histories, biographies, nature writing, and more. Thanks to Carolyn Hotchkiss, Laura Capaldini, and John and Ingrid Hotchkiss for our "meta" conversations about writing, superb book recommendations, and ongoing encouragement.

My children, Emily and Mark, have inherited the same genes. They happily discuss books, authors, and writing techniques with me, and pass along references and research to support my crazy obsession with nonfiction writing. My husband, Steve, is my ideal reader and personal anchor; we read and share books, and his advice helps keep this whole endeavor on the rails.

Finally, to all the nonfiction writers who plug away, showing us the world around us in a new light, or the world beyond our own circles: Thank you, and keep on writing.

NOTES

1 Hope Jahren, *Lab Girl* (New York: Alfred A. Knopf, 2016).

2 Hunter Gelbach et al, "Creating birds of similar feathers: Leveraging similarity to improve teacher-student relationships and academic achievement," *Journal of Educational Psychology*, 108, 342–352.

3 Chai M. Tyng, Hafeez U. Amin, Mohamad N. M. Saad, and Aamir S. Malik, "The Influences of Emotion on Learning and Memory," *Frontiers in Psychology* v. 8, August 2017 (Published online August 24, 2017).

4 The quote comes from an interview Sherry Turkle did with *MIT News* published November 17, 2015, titled "3 Questions: Sherry Turkle on 'Reclaiming Conversation.'" It is the subject of her book *Reclaiming Conversation* (New York: Penguin, 2015).

5 Chip Heath and Dan Heath, "The Curse of Knowledge," *Harvard Business Review*, December 2006.

6 The quote comes from an article Hossenfelder published in the online publication Aeon.co, titled "What I learned as a hired consultant to autodidact physicists." I checked with Hossenfelder, and she stands by her words.

7 Leonid Rozenblit and Frank Keil, "The Misunderstood Limits of Folk Science: An Illusion of Explanatory Depth," *Cognitive Science* 26.5 (2002): 521–562.

8 Daniel Levitin, *A Field Guide to Lies* (New York: Dutton, 2016).

9 For the definite, academic explanation of the topic, check out this book: Harry G. Frankfurt, *On Bullshit* (Princeton: Princeton University Press, 2009).

10 Assess your own need for closure at this site: http://Terpconnect.umd.edu/~hannahk/NFC_Scale.html

11 I first encountered this fascinating research in Jamie Holmes's book *Nonsense*. (See the bibliography.) The original article by Frenkel-Brunswick, which is hard to dig up, was published in 1948 in the *Journal of Personality* (volume 18), with the title "Intolerance of Ambiguity as an Emotional and Perceptual Personality Variable."

12 Michele Wucker, *The Gray Rhino* (New York: St. Martin's Press, 2016).

13 For more on moral taste buds see Jonathan Haidt, *The Righteous Mind: Why Good People are Divided by Politics and Religion* (New York: Pantheon, 2012).

14 Dennis Overbye, "Physicists Find Elusive Particle Seen as Key to Universe," *New York Times*, July 4, 2012.

15 George Loewenstein, "The psychology of curiosity: a review and reinterpretation," *Psychological Bulletin*, 116(1), 75–98.

16 Jordan Litman, "Curiosity and the pleasures of learning," *Cognition and Emotion*, 19 (2005), 793–814.

17 Mario Livio, *Why: What Makes Us Curious* (New York: Simon and Schuster, 2017).

18 For more insight on headlines from BuzzFeed itself, check out the article "18 Clever Tips for Writing Headlines That'll Make People Feel Things," by Carolyn Kylstra, January 22, 2016.

19 John Medina, *Brain Rules* (Seattle: Pear Press, 2014).

20 Cursory research (Wikipedia) indicates that the Dutch captain Willem de Vlamingh encountered black swans on the Swan River (which he named) in January 1697. Of course, black swans would have been no surprise to the natives of Australia at that time. Metaphors clearly rely on cultural context.

21 Jonathan Haidt, *The Happiness Hypothesis: Finding Modern Truth in Ancient Wisdom* (New York: Basic Books, 2006).

22 Check out the Metamania database at meta-phorlab.org/metamia-a-free-database-of-analogy-and-metaphor/. The organization also hosts an annual conference, the Metaphor Festival, dedicated to the use of figurative language. If you're in Amsterdam, check it out and let me know what it's like.

23 Michael Gazzinaga, *Who's in Charge: Free Will and the Science of the Brain* (New York: Ecco, 2011).

24 Listen to Uri Hasson describing his own research on his TED talk: www.ted.com/speakers/uri_hasson.

25 Robert Sapolsky, *Behave: The Biology of Humans at our Best and Worst* (New York: Penguin Books, 2017).

26 Daniel Coyle, *The Culture Code: The Secrets of Highly Successful Groups* (New York: Bantam Books, 2018).

27 Poornima Vijayashanker and Karen Catlin, *Present! A Techie's Guide to Public Speaking* (CreateSpace, 2015).

28 Hope Jahren, *Lab Girl* (New York: Alfred A. Knopf, 2016).

29 N.J. Enfield, *How We Talk: The Inner Workings of Conversation* (New York: Basic books, 2017).

30 You can try SCIgen on the lab's website: https://pdos.csail.mit.edu/archive/scigen/.

31 Richard Van Noorden, "Publishers withdraw more than 120 gibberish papers" *Nature News*, February 24, 2014.

32 I realize that fMRI data and interpretation may be flawed. We cannot necessarily be certain that brain activity seen on these scans isn't spurious. But this is a book about writing, not brain surgery, so I hope you'll take the addition of research as it was intended—to reinforce good writing habits.

33 Corrie Goldman, "This Is Your Brain on Austen," *Stanford Report*, September 7, 2012.

34 For a description of this metaphor study, refer to the Stanford News article by Adam Gorlick, "Is crime a virus or a beast? When describing crime, Stanford study shows the word you pick can frame the debate on how to fight it," *Stanford Report*, February 23, 2011.

35 Find this and other intentionally egregious misuses of analogy on the Bulwer-Lytton Fiction Contest website: www.bulwer-lytton.com.

36 Daniel Oppenheimer, "Consequences of Erudite Vernacular Utilized Irrespective of Necessity: Problems with Using Long Words Needlessly," *Applied Cognitive Psychology*, 20: 139–156 (2006).

37 Jonathan Haidt, The Righteous Mind: Why Good People are Divided by Politics and Religion (New York: Pantheon, 2012)

38 Adam Grant, *Give and Take: A Revolutionary Approach to Success* (New York: Viking, 2013)

39 Aronson, Willerman, and Floyd, "The effect of a pratfall on increasing interpersonal attractiveness," *Psychonomic Science*, 4(6), 227–228.

40 Thomas Veatch, "A Theory of Humor," *International Journal of Humor Research*, 11/2, 161–216.

41 Peter McGraw and Joel Warner, *The Humor Code: A Global Search for What Makes Things Funny* (New York: Simon and Schuster, 2014).

42 Jamie Holmes, *Nonsense: The Power of Not Knowing*, (New York: Crown Publishing Group, 2014).

43 Neil deGrasse Tyson, *Astrophysics for People in a Hurry* (New York: W.W. Norton, 2017).

44 Wiley-Blackwell, "Humor Plays an Important Role in Healthcare Even When Patients Are Terminally Ill," *Science Daily*, April 9, 2008.

45 Dan Ariely and Jeff Kreisler, *Dollars and Sense: How We Misthink Money and How to Spend Smarter*, (New York: Harper, 2017).

46 Francis-Noël Thomas and Mark Turner, *Clear and Simple as the Truth: Writing Classic Prose* (Princeton: Princeton University Press, 2011).

SELECTED BIBLIOGRAPHY AND RECOMMENDED READING

Alda, Alan. *If I Understood You, Would I Have This Look on My Face?* New York: Random House, 2017.

Carey, Benedict. *How We Learn: The Surprising Truth About When, Where, and Why It Happens.* New York: Random House, 2014.

Carr, Nicholas. *The Shallows: What the Internet is Doing to Our Brains.* New York: W.W. Norton, 2010.

Enfield, N.J. *How We Talk: The Inner Workings of Conversation.* New York: Basic Books, 2017.

Eyal, Nir and Hoover, Ryan. *Hooked: How to Build Habit-Forming Products.* New York: Portfolio, 2014.

Frankfurt, Harry G. *On Bullshit.* Princeton: Princeton University Press, 2005.

Grant, Adam. *Give and Take: A Revolutionary Approach to Success.* New York: Viking, 2013.

Gray, Dave. *Liminal Thinking: Create the Change You Want by Changing the Way You Think.* Brooklyn: Two Waves Books, 2016.

Haidt, Jonathan. *The Happiness Hypothesis: Finding Modern Truth in Ancient Wisdom.* New York: Basic Books, 2006.

————. *The Righteous Mind: Why Good People Are Divided by Politics and Religion.* New York: Pantheon, 2012.

Heath, Chip and Dan. *Switch: How to Change Things When Change Is Hard.* New York: Crown Business, 2010.

Holmes, Jamie. *Nonsense: The Power of Not Knowing.* New York: Crown Publishers, 2015.

Kahneman, Daniel. *Thinking Fast and Slow.* New York: Farrar, Straus and Giroux, 2011.

Levitin, Daniel. *A Field Guide to Lies: Critical Thinking in the Information Age.* New York: Dutton, 2016.

Livio, Mario. *Why: What Makes Us Curious.* New York: Simon and Schuster, 2017.

McGraw, Peter and Warner, Joel. *The Humor Code: A Global Search for What Makes Things Funny.* New York: Simon and Schuster, 2014.

McPhee, John. *Draft No. 4: On the Writing Process.* New York: Farrar, Straus and Giroux, 2017.

McRaney, David. *You Are Not So Smart: Why You Have Too Many Friends on Facebook, Why Your Memory Is Mostly Fiction, and 46 Other Ways You're Deluding Yourself.* New York: Dutton, 2011.

Medina, John. *Brain Rules: 12 Principles for Surviving and Thriving at Work, Home, and School.* Seattle: Pear Press, 2014.

Pinker, Steven. *The Language Instinct: How the Mind Creates Language*. New York: William Morrow, 1993.

————. *The Sense of Style: The Thinking Person's Guide to Writing in the 21st Century*. New York: Viking, 2014.

Sapolsky, Robert. *Behave: The Biology of Humans at our Best and Worst*. New York: Penguin, 2017.

Sloman, Steven and Fernbach, Philip. *The Knowledge Illusion: Why We Never Think Alone*. New York: Riverhead Books, 2017.

Thomas, Francis-Noël and Turner, Mark. *Clear and Simple as the Truth: Writing Classic Prose*. Princeton: Princeton University Press, 2011.

Vijayashanker, Poornima and Catlin, Karen. *Present! A Techie's Guide to Public Speaking*. CreateSpace, 2015.

Wilson, Timothy D. *Strangers to Ourselves: Discovering the Adaptive Unconscious*. New York: Belknap Press, 2002.

INDEX

ABOUT THE AUTHOR

Anne Janzer is an award-winning author on a mission to help writers communicate more effectively.

As a freelance marketing writer, she worked with more than a hundred technology businesses, from industry giants to innovative start-ups, helping them articulate positioning and messaging in crowded markets. Today she shares writing practices through online courses, blog posts, and, of course, books.

Her book *The Writer's Process: Getting Your Brain in Gear* combines the lessons of a writing career with the teachings of cognitive science to uncover the secrets of writing productivity. *The Workplace Writer's Process* shares the secrets to setting yourself up for success when writing in an organization, based on lessons learned in the field.

Anne wrote *Subscription Marketing: Strategies for Nurturing Customers in a World of Churn* to help marketers manage the disruptions of the subscription economy. Now in its second edition, *Subscription Marketing* has also been translated into Japanese.

Anne is a graduate of Stanford University. To find out what she's up to next, visit her website: annejanzer.com.

24234917R00124

Made in the USA
Columbia, SC
20 August 2018